The Joy
of
Creation and Success

The Joy
of
Creation and Success

Author
Ajay Srivastava

Jyotirvid, Jyotirvisharad

Published by:

Ajay Kumar Srivastava

45, Awas Vikas Colony, Betiya Hata,

Gorakhpur – 273001 (U.P.), India

Mobile No.: +91-9867837184

First Edition, 2023

Disclaimer: This publication contains the opinions and ideas of its author and is designed to provide useful information in regard to the subject matter covered. The author and the publisher specifically disclaim any responsibility for liability, loss, or risk, personal or otherwise, that is incurred as a consequence, directly or indirectly, of the use and application of any of the contents of this book.

Lord Sun

Prayer

ॐ भास्कराय विद्महे मार्त्तण्डाय धीमहि तन्नः सूर्यः प्रचोदयात्।।

‖ Om Bhaskaray Vidmahe Martanday Dheemahi

Tanah Surya Prachodayat ‖

(**Translation**: Let me meditate on the Sun God, the maker of the day. Let the Sun God grant me higher intellect and illuminate my mind.)

Dedication

I dedicate this book to my father (Late) Sri R.A.L Srivastava who taught me to be an independent, courageous and determined person, and my mother Maya Srivastava whose unconditional love and support always help me to overcome all the obstacles in my life. She has a selfless spirit and served others throughout her life. Her immense patience is peerless and she always inspires me to go ahead.

Preface

Creation and success is a journey, and travelling on this path is not easy in life. The seed of writing something on this subject had been dormant in my mind for many years, but once I was travelling it germinates.

While meeting with different types of people on that journey and observing their behaviour, I analyzed that some of them are always interested in getting something without any hard work and they feel very happy if they get it for free. They are always interested in taking shortcuts to get succeed.

In my experience I have seen that such kind of people gradually lose the power to do anything constructive in their life. Accepting always freebies makes them a coward. Their greed comes first while taking any decision and they are not ready to compromise with their comfort. They always take decisions on the back foot in their life; therefore, they fail in their endeavour.

Creation is a long journey and it is not limited to a few thoughts and chapters. The chapters in this book are my thoughts and experience and I feel that these are the essential steps that a person should follow before starting his journey to do something constructive in his life.

In this book, I explained deeply, what are those necessary steps a person has to take if he wants to do something constructive in his life. Everyone wants to enjoy the fruit of creation, everyone wants to enjoy the fragrance of beautiful flowers, but these fruits and flowers and not available in the market, it is a journey and you can enjoy such things if you will walk on a certain path.

 I have explained how to travel on these paths and what necessary steps and measures you should take to reach your destination.

I give special thanks to my younger brother Abhay Srivastava and my uncle Chandra Bhoosan Srivastava for their valuable suggestions, without which such work would not have been possible.

I bow to God for completing this book. Without the grace of the Almighty, it is not possible for me to express my thoughts in words.

Ajay Srivastava

22nd April 2022

Navi Mumbai

Acknowledgement

The existence of this book would not have been possible without the help of my wife Seema and my daughter Saanvi. They provided me enough help to write down my thoughts which I have collected so far in my life. My wife has been instrumental as an illustrator and proof-reader and has given me enough insights to write the matter in a simple and explanatory manner.

Ajay Srivastava

Contents

Chapter 1

Introduction

* **What is Creation?**

* **Creation is joy, Creation is happiness, Creation is ecstasy.**

Only those who engage themselves in the activity of creation can experience the real joy in their lives that does not come from any other source of entertainment.

When a child makes something out of his cardboard, innocent happiness is clearly visible on his face. When he builds his palace out of the playing cards then he is filled with immense joy, even though it may fall soon but the joy of creation is unparalleled and cannot be compared with any other joy. When a sculptor makes an idol, when a person sees a beautiful flower in a garden that he has planted they get wonderful pleasure. Everything you create fills you with immense joy. The feeling of being a mother when a woman gives birth to a child is utterly incomparable.

When a person selflessly thinks of creating something, then only that thought takes the person to the next level of maturity.

- Now such a person's mind starts thinking creatively and positive waves start to surround him.

- Now that person is going to give something to humanity, and when he engages in that act and moves forward, his whole structure starts changing.

- Now he is going to contribute something to the work of "God - The Greatest Creator" whose creation is going on continuously.

When a person starts using his energy for such creative purposes then enormous positive energy starts supporting him, such types of people do not deviate from the obstacles coming on their path. Obstacles are part of the growth and the surrounded positive energy has strong power to wipe out all the obstacles. Now, such a person is no longer an ordinary person, he has become a servant of the "Greatest Creator".

Just as creative qualities take one to the next level of consciousness, destructive activities and thinking destroy the possibility of consciousness rising. When a person thinks that I will destroy this thing, I will abuse someone, I will quarrel with someone, I will kill that person, etc. Even though he has not done so, with such thinking he makes his own way to go down in life. We create our own heaven and hell by our thoughts and actions, and our every thought and action of creation or destruction prepares that path for us.

Just as creative qualities take a person to a higher level, similarly destructive qualities make a person more inhuman and there is no limit to go up or down in this human life, and the decision to choose the direction is entirely in our hands and our every thought and action is creating steps in that direction.

When a person thinks that I will do something creative, I will contribute something for the betterment of humanity and engages in doing some constructive work. Then people may say that he is doing that work for others, but in reality, what he seems to be doing for others is not doing for others but he is doing it for himself. In this way, he is raising his soul to the next level of maturity and gradually he is coming closer to the "Greatest Creator".

When a person involves himself in an act of destruction, he thinks that I am causing destruction to others but in reality, he is causing destruction to himself. Now, he has chosen his path to go down, to hell, and he alone is responsible for all the suffering in his life.

Such a person has lost the innocent happiness that little children feel by building a palace of cards. He forgets that when a small child rejoices in a small creation, what pleasure will he attain when he will become a servant of the "Greatest Creator" and engages himself in the process of creation and progresses gradually on the path of upward direction.

But people are so miser that they never want to give anything to others, the act of doing is a faraway thing, they never think about doing anything constructive in life, but in return, they want all the happiness in their life.

Their destruction work starts from morning itself; they are ready to abuse others on any matter, and many of them without using abusive words won't say a single word. They get ready to quarrel on any trivial matter and start shouting for hours in the office or at home on any issue. For instance, many people indulge in quarrelsome activities;

- When they just have simple conversations at the table

- When they eat at the dining table

- When they walk down the street and look for a chance to argue or fight with someone

They are full of destructive energy and just wait for a chance to destroy something. When they are unable to find anything to destroy, they start plucking leaves, grass, and plants. They start throwing stuff here and there. They are ready to fight on the streets for hours just for a minor scratch on their car. They don't know that by indulging in all such activities, they are wasting their time and energy and that is limited in every person's life.

Every day they sow the seeds of destruction and by and by all these seeds are making their way to go down, they themselves are responsible for the creation of their own hell. On the contrary, they seek all the happiness in their life and when their life does not provide, they start demanding from others. They seek happiness from their wife, they look for it among their friends, and bitterness begins to creep into their relationships because the one who asks is always perceived as weaker, and people tend to distance themselves from those who constantly ask for things. They try every possible way to buy happiness with money. They search for happiness from other sources, and that is why entertainment has become such a huge business these days.

If you are not thinking in a constructive manner then you are putting yourself in the opposite direction of the elevation of your soul. This is the journey of upward and downward direction which every human being is doing. The downward journey is always easy, the upward journey is always tough and this is the tendency of our mind to choose always an easy path. If you have not chosen an upward journey then by default you are going in a downward direction.

Our every thought of creation no matter how big or small it is, contributes something on the path of joy and happiness. Now, such a person has started sowing his seeds on the path of creation, and one day his path will meet with the path of "The Ultimate Creator".

Jesus said – "Truly, I say to you, unless you turn and become like children, you will never enter the kingdom of heaven."

Key Points

- Always think in a constructive manner and involve yourself in the process of creation, no matter how big or small but your steps are important.

- If you sow the seeds of destruction, you cannot get pleasure in your life.

- Select the upward journey in life otherwise by default you are going in a downward direction.

Chapter 2

Creation and Success

Only a person full of positive energy can do something constructive in his life. There are many challenges in the path of creation. So, many people only think and discuss to do something in their life, but they are not ready to take any step further because they are afraid of challenges. When you move in any direction, you have to face resistance.

There are many resistance and speed breakers come when driving a car on the road. A person always has to keep an eye on the road while driving, his eyes are constantly on alert until he reaches the destination, his hands control the steering and provide direction to the car and his feet control the accelerator and the brake. The need can come at any time and he has to sit alert only then he can reach his destination.

The above example is very simple to understand as we are used to it. The same principle applies when a person starts his journey to do something creative in his life. He has to start the journey alone where the path is completely unknown. He has to clear the pebbles on the roads, which means he has to take care of the speed and overcome the obstacles on the path. He has to show his alertness every time like a driver cannot sleep, similarly, such a person cannot keep his mind in the sleep zone till he reaches the destination.

He has to select the direction very carefully on these unknown paths where there are not any signboards. He should be courageous enough to face the obstacles and not feel frustrated when his vehicle gets stuck in a traffic jam (serious obstacles) and its speed gets slow.

As a vehicle, the pace of life is never the same. Sometimes its speed is high, sometimes its speed is slow, sometimes it has to face a speed breaker, and sometimes it gets stuck in jam. While travelling in a car and proceeding toward our destination, we don't complain and don't get disheartened when the speed gets slow or it stuck in a jam because we know that the situation will not remain the same, it will change soon.

Many times, we face such types of situations while travelling, but when such things start happening in life, people feel frustrated and they start taking tablets of depression because they are not ready to accept that their journey of life which was running fast, suddenly slows down. Now it is facing resistance and there seems to be no end to speed breakers, it seems that the journey has frozen now.

They start comparing it with other vehicles which are running fast. Many of them start saying, "Look, I overtook other cars several miles back, but now this one has overtaken me, and I'm stuck in such a mess that there's no way out."

They forget that they still have a brain that has decision-making power, they have eyes that can identify paths, their hands are still on the steering to select the direction and their feet can still run and has the ability to control the accelerator and brakes. Don't forget that your vehicle is still intact and now has become much stronger.

Just as no traffic jam stays on the road forever, in the same manner, life always moves on. The person who understands how to drive a vehicle properly, a person who knows when to use the accelerator and when to use the brakes, ultimately reaches his destination. A person who is always attentive because a small mistake can lead to an accident. A person who does not despair when the vehicle of his life gets stuck in a traffic jam, but he has the ability to pull him out of such situations, and not drop him in the middle of the way. Only such a person can do something constructive in his life.

What is the meaning of success in life?

Success is a personal thing; the definition of success depends on the perception of the individual. While one person feels successful after achieving something, for others it may be a waste of time and energy. Success in life means feeling satisfaction with whatever a person has in his hands, an aspiring person cannot be called successful because this race is not going to end anywhere. After getting one thing, the desire to get another thing is born immediately.

A person runs after what is not in his hands and thinks that after achieving such a thing, he will become a successful person, but the thing becomes useless as soon as it comes into his hands. Many people can say that such a person is very successful because he has a lot of wealth or he has a lot of fame in society. However, such information from any mouth provides more about the speaker's view, and less about the person concerned. In fact, he is saying that only money and fame are important in his life and that his eyes are only following such a thing. Whereas, it may be possible that a person who has acquired so much wealth or fame is highly dissatisfied and his mind starts racing to get those things that he does not have.

As time passes the definition of success changes, it changes for every individual, it changes for the society, it changes for the country. So, if you are satisfied with your existence without comparing with others then you are a successful person. You are yourself and remember 'God' took nine months to create you. For nine months, nature has been continuously and silently working on your mother's womb, only then such a creation has taken place. Like a sculptor works continuously to make a beautiful idol but this idol is alive because "The Sculptor Himself is God".

In this court called life, you are the judge, you are the lawyer and you are the culprit. Therefore, there is no point in feeling dissatisfied by comparing yourself with others. When you drive your car on the road you will find that there are always some vehicles in front of your car and some behind your car and all of them are going towards their respective destination.

You cannot overtake everyone and you cannot be behind everyone and you will get the same situation again whenever you drive your vehicle on the road. So, if someone overtakes you, let them do so because their destination is different, they have to achieve something else in their life and they may be in a hurry to get there, and that is not your destination. Everyone here has a different destination, so the time and speed required to reach it will be different for each person. Therefore, there is no point in feeling dissatisfied by comparing yourself with others.

A weak-minded person compares himself with others. He wants instant success and is not ready to work hard and wait for it. An impatient person wants everything quickly, and when he doesn't get it, he gets depressed and gives up his goal. But a wise person knows that it takes time to get results. A wise person who has the virtue of patience never compares himself with others.

"What we are today comes from our thoughts of yesterday, and present thoughts build our life of tomorrow: our life is the creation of our own mind." – Lord Buddha

<u>Key Points</u>

- Positive energy is required on the path of creation, hence a person should remove every kind of negativity from his life.

- The path of creation tests your patience, an impatient person soon leaves the path because he wants the fruits immediately after sowing the seeds.

- Success in life means feeling satisfaction with whatever a person has in his hands, an aspiring person cannot be called successful because this race is not going to end anywhere.

- If someone overtakes you don't compare yourself with him, everyone's destination is different here, so their timing and speed are different.

- A wise person who has the virtue of patience never compares himself with others.

Chapter 3

Power of Giving

* **Why should we give?**

* **What should we give?**

* **What will we get if we give?**

When a person thinks about giving something, immediately the above questions start coming to his mind. There is no direct benefit visible when we give something to others. Our mind will say what is the necessity of being so generous. Are you a fool? To fulfill their materialistic desire people are always ready to take from others, they are ready to deceit, they are ready to strangle others, they are ready to rob, they are ready to kill, they are ready to do anything to get something but not ready to give anything, and if anything is available free of cost, then they are very happy to accept it.

People rush to the streets when they hear that something is available there for free. They feel happy with such information that nothing is getting out of their hands and getting something for free. They say, what a good chance that wishes are being fulfilled without any cost. Am I a stupid person to miss out such a chance? People are so empty inside that they are ready to take anything if it is available free of cost.

But remember nothing is available free of cost in this world, and if a person is offering something free then there must be some hidden meaning behind that which is currently not visible, but there's some meaning hidden in that giving and when you accept such a thing you are developing a relationship with the giver. In these scenarios, do not confuse it with something you receive selflessly from others like any birthday or marriage gift, but you must understand the purpose behind it and know that there is no hidden meaning behind such an offer.

If you are accepting any costly item then you are creating a relationship with the giver and now you are one step behind the giver. By accepting it you have lost the quality of patience and put your temptation first. If you have any desire for that then you should have earned such items through your hard work, but you have not done that, you have put forward your desire first and pushed your soul back.

Your every act of pushing your soul back shrinks it. Such people slowly lose their courage and always feel intimidated because they have not done any work to develop their soul and have always given preference to their temptation. When the opportunity comes to develop their soul, they push it back and are ready to accept anything for free, ready to deceit, ready to rob, and choose to leave their soul behind every time. When the soul is not developed it cannot think about creating something. Only a courageous and evolved soul has the potential to create something in this life.

3.1 You Are Developing a Relation

When you accept anything from others, you are developing a relationship with them. Selflessly, when people give gifts to their friends, their relatives, colleagues, or someone they love, such kind of activity is developing a relationship with the other person. Once you pay for that the relationship is closed.

When you accept anything for free, you are developing a relationship between yourself and the giver. You don't know but after your acceptance, the relationship has developed. Companies know this principle, so before launching any product it is necessary to distribute it for free. After your acceptance, the relationship has been formed, and now this relationship starts spreading slowly among a number of people. This is why the principle of free distribution works, and for those who have accepted it, the company is no longer a stranger to them. This free product in their house will affect their mind and every time they see it, involuntarily they remember it. This invisible band will pull the person to use the same product over and over again, and now the bonding will continue.

In the same manner, the freely available information on the internet is also not free. If you learn something by watching any video on the internet and you think you got it free then you are wrong. Remember, nothing is free here, now you have developed a relationship between the provider and yourself. The next time when the provider introduces a product in the market, it will be very difficult for you to refuse it because there is invisible bondage that has been developed between both of you, and now you know that such a product is not coming from an unknown person. Now a trust has been developed between you and the provider.

But the question is how this principle works in the theory of creation, it seems there is no relation between acceptance of anything free and creativity. But when we see deep then we will find that there is a strong relationship between these two.

When you accept anything free of cost then your soul shrinks, you have lost the courage to get that by paying it. No matter, it would take some time to get it in your hands, but you should choose the opportunity to develop patience, courage, and spirit. When you receive something by paying for it, you have developed your soul to become more courageous and more patient.

But who wants to reject such things that are coming free? People commit various crimes to get some stuff in their hands without paying for it. They keep filling their homes with possessions and emptying their soul. Not knowing that their soul begins to shrink and they start losing their courage, gradually they become so frightened and immediately feel terrified of any news that they are losing something out of their hands. I have seen that such people get so angry even on jokes that someone will say that you are about to lose something. Accepting freebies every day fills their house but empties their soul.

Such people have chosen the path of emptying their soul in their life and they are far away from the path of creation. They may have resources in their life. They discuss doing something new and innovative, they discuss creating something unique, and they feel the power of their resources but they forget the first step, a shrunken soul cannot create anything.

3.2 Giving is an Asset

Human life is unpredictable, we don't know what is going to happen next moment. When we help others, when we give something to others without our personal interest, we create an asset. Our intention to help someone, timely help, and the nature of help are more important than the quantity of help. Giving is an asset and such wealth gets deposited in the invisible hands of nature. When the time comes this repository opens up, then what you have given without your personal interest comes back to help you multifold.

Once I and my friend Suresh were travelling with our families from Mumbai to worship an old Lord Shiva temple in a hilly area. But in the middle of the forest and hilly terrain, my car broke down. It was getting dark and the temple site was about 30 km from there, we start looking around for some help. We saw a house at the bottom of the hill and we went there. The owner of the house has come out and we told him about our problem. He immediately called some villagers and everyone pulled my car in front of his house. He arranged his vehicle for us and said you can go to the temple and stay overnight there and have darshan of Lord Shiva in the morning after that you can come with a mechanic and take your car.

He didn't ask us for any extra money, just asked to pay the cost of diesel. We were surprised that he could have demanded some extra money from us and we had no other option but to pay but he didn't. The next morning after darshan we discussed the problem with the car mechanic but they told us that we need to pull the vehicle to the nearby city as maintenance of the car will take time. We reached a nearby town and informed the car insurance company about towing the car. The insurance company said that the towing vehicle would be available soon and the driver would wait for you at the entry point of that hilly area which was about 15 km from our present location. We decided to send our families to Mumbai by bus, we reached the local bus stand and got tickets to Mumbai for our families. Immediately the bus arrived and we made our families sit on the bus, then both of us took a deep breath that now we were ready to solve the problem of the car.

That was a very small town and no taxi or vehicle was available to go to the entry point of the hill where our towing vehicle was coming. We asked several drivers to take us there, but none of them were willing to go. One traffic policeman was watching our activities, he asked us what is the problem. We explained that we need to go to that entry point but no vehicle is available. He told us not to worry, that is a remote point so these drivers are not taking an interest, he will arrange a vehicle for us because he knows which vehicle goes in that direction, till then we both can sit below the fan in the police station. Soon, he arranged a vehicle and instructed the driver that drops us off at that point and not to charge any extra money. The driver replied do not worry he will do so.

We thanked the policeman and sat in the vehicle then the driver discussed with us why are we going to that location. We said that a towing vehicle is coming and we will go to get our car up that hill. He asked if I know any car garages in this city, I said no we don't know. Then he said that there is a car garage nearby, if you want, we can go there and you can discuss your point with the garage owner. I said okay, drive your vehicle to that place. The place was nearby and within minutes we reached there. We discussed the matter with the garage owner and said when we return it will be night, garage owner replied don't worry if you come late at night our staff will wait for you, and he will make all necessary arrangements for spare parts which our car may need.

After that, we reached the entry point of the hill wherethe towing vehicle was already waiting for us, we thanked the driver and tried to pay some extra money for his help but he refused. After a few hours of traveling, we reached the front of the house where we parked our car, the driver tied my car to the towing vehicle, we thanked the owner of the house and after a few hours of traveling, we reached the garage.

It was 11 o'clock at the night, the owner of the garage was about to leave and we saw some laborers waiting for us. The owner said I am leaving and these workers will repair your vehicle at night but you have to pay him the fee for working at night. I said no problem I will pay for that but how long will it take, he replied that it will take at least 6 hours, and asked did you guys have any food. I said no, today we are just travelling from one place to another. He immediately gave me the keys of his motorcycle and said there is a very nice restaurant here, take my bike and go there, eat your food, these staff will repair your car by morning. We both took his motorcycle and reached that restaurant. We were both very hungry and we found that the food was really delicious. During dinner, we were discussing help from all the unknown persons whom we met for the first time and since that incident, we never met them. My friend said that it seems that the script of such happenings has already been written, otherwise, who thinks that the one who has come to the garage at 11 pm has eaten something or not.

We finished our meal and reached the garage and saw the workers doing their work. I also noticed that another vehicle had arrived which was not there when we reached the garage with our car. I inquired about that vehicle, workers said its owner comes here often, right now he just parked his vehicle for some maintenance, and tomorrow he will come to pick it up. I said if you don't mind, can we both take a rest for a few hours in this car as there is no place to sit here till morning. The main worker said no problem and he opened the gate. We both rested there for the next few hours till our car was ready.

It was dawn, my friend was driving, and I was contemplating the entire situation and feeling utterly amazed by all the help we had received from these strangers, whom I didn't know and whom I never saw again. Our car was speeding down the highway, the sun's rays spreading across the horizon; it wasn't an ordinary morning for me. My mind was now engrossed in trying to understand the workings of nature's unseen forces.

3.3 Acceptance is an Obligation

When a person accepts anything then he obliges to do that thing. When a person always wants to take something, when a person is always interested in taking free gifts and when a person is not interested in giving anything to others. Then such a person is creating a heavy burden of responsibility on his shoulders, and with this heavy stones, it would become very difficult for him to do anything constructive in his life.

Whatever burden they have put on their shoulders, it is their responsibility to fulfill them first. Your acceptance is an obligation that creates burden on your shoulders. It is not possible for such a person to take on any new assignment when he is already loaded with previous assignments. A person whose shoulders are already loaded cannot take steps on the path of creation.

Therefore, it is necessary for such a person to fulfill previous obligations and close all open accounts before starting the process of opening another new account. Your every acceptance is opening an account and it is creating an imbalance in your life's balance sheet because your debit side is increasing.

No matter how many qualities you have, your life vehicle will not move forward, if you will burden your shoulders with your deeds and make a mountain of responsibilities in front.

The path of creation is for those who have very less burden on their shoulders. Those who have more assets and very less debt on their life's balance sheet can take steps on this path. Whatever the assets you have generated all those will help you to move forward and your every obligation will tie your feet and hold you back from taking any constructive action.

3.4 Giving and Expansion

"Strength is Life, Weakness is Death. Expansion is Life, Contraction is Death. Love is Life, Hatred is Death." - Swami Vivekananda

Expansion is the nature of every soul and for this purpose, it has taken birth on the planet earth. A person feels happy when he does an activity to expand something, when he does cultivation, when he learns a new skill or when he teaches something to someone, etc. These are all the activities of expansion and because of this expansion humanity continues on earth. The birth of a child is the expansion of life. Any activity of expansion makes one experience joy in life – "Expansion is bliss, Shrinking is misery". When a person participated in the act of expansion, he developed something deep in his soul. When a person supports shrinking, he loses something in his soul.

When a person commits any act of destruction for his personal gain his soul shrinks, outside he may look like a very courageous person but every act of destruction creates fear within, because his soul begins to shrink. The more fearful he becomes, the more he seeks security in every matter of his life. I have seen that such a person always ask questions related to security, even in those matters where there is no question of asking such questions.

In my corporate career, I have seen that the person who always gives pain to others becomes so fearful and looks for security in every sphere of life. Such kinds of people do not accept to eat any food offered by their colleagues or friends while having lunch. While sitting on the chair, at first, they check whether everything is fine or not, they are always afraid to fall down. They want to collect all information about their colleagues, surrounding persons, and others but keep all their information in the dark.

They are always fearful and do not trust anyone. What they are doing, they are looking for security in every aspect of their life. Every act of destruction and causing pain to others gives birth to such a fearful person. He may think that whatever act he is doing is the right act but in reality, his soul starts shrinking, and remember a shrunken soul cannot do any type of constructive work in life.

During the second world war, Hitler did a lot of destruction to the world. But, in reality he was a very timid person, he was always afraid of having poison in the food, so, he could not eat his food without being tasted by another person. His spirit had shrunk.

The more you do the destruction and give pain to others the more your soul shrinks and gradually you lose all your power of creation. Now such type of person has chosen a path to go down in his life.

Expansion is the nature of every soul and we always think of expansion in our life. When the expansion on earth becomes limited, people begin to explore the universe. What is the underlying desire of all these thoughts and activities, it is nothing but an expansion, and the ultimate goal of this inherent desire, one day the soul finds out the reason for this vast expansion which is called 'The Universe'.

3.5 Giving and Courage

Every activity of expansion requires courage. Without courage, you cannot expand anything, and giving is that virtue that makes you more courageous. To leave something from your hands requires a lot of courage and only the owner of the thing has the power to give it. When you leave something, when you give something to someone, you become the owner, such activity gives expansion to your soul and the person becomes a more courageous person. When you accept something, your soul shrinks because the giver is always bigger and the taker is always smaller. Each time when you will accept items to fulfill your greed, your soul shrinks, and each time you will lose your courage.

People who accept free items or are always on the lookout for free items / gifts in their life gradually become so fearful and immediately get panic about any trivial information. Such type of people always prefers all types of comfort in every sphere of their life. They always look for the most comfortable place to sit and do not bother to give their seat to anyone even if a very old and sick man is standing beside them. For them, their comfort first, they are not ready to compromise with their comfort and do not hesitate to put others in trouble, but their demand must be fulfilled at first. They are a fearful person, with every act of acceptance of freebies, not giving anything to others, and taking interest in acts of destruction, they have chosen the path to shrink their soul.

They do everything against the nature of the soul to fulfill their materialistic desires. Such people cannot make any kind of creation in their life, no matter how much deep pockets they have and how many people they are controlling. They always think on the back foot and act only when the situation is completely safe and turns in their favor. They fail in every activity of expansion and later wonder why they didn't succeed in their venture even after putting so much time, money, and effort.

When life provides them the opportunity to expand, they did not develop their mind and soul. At every opportunity they stepped back, they were always interested in taking something and always refusing to give anything, they always chose the most comfortable place to sit and never thought about sharing it with someone in need. Every act they selected to shrink in their life and now looking for expansion with their resources. Though these are essential but not the only things and something else is needed. The quality of a person comes first for any creation.

When you give something, you feel something great in your heart. Doing the act of charity, giving food to the hungry people, even when you plant a seed, you are contributing something in the act of expansion because you are providing an opportunity for a seed to become a tree. Doing an act of gardening or plantation or giving someone a gift on an occasion or providing some guidance to a person who is looking for some valuable suggestion. In our day-to-day life, at various times our life provides opportunities for expansion of our soul and to become a more courageous person. Because only a courageous soul can engage itself in the process of creation.

The person who always chooses every action to shrink his soul, cannot do any kind of creation in his life. When life offers you an opportunity to expand, don't hold it back, accept it with full courage. Creation is a journey to the unknown that requires a lot of courage. Every selfless giving count here, no matter whether it is small or big, but it contributes something to the development of your soul.

3.6 Be Cautious Before Giving

Giving is an asset but it requires careful observation. It is good to be charitable but people may take unnecessary advantage of your generous nature. It is good to donate to needy people but people can show you their double faces to cheat you. Everyone appreciates the donation but it is only for the needy people. You need to check whether the person is looking for help, really needs them, or has some hidden motive behind it. The decision to give completely depends on the discretion of the donor which each person takes according to his/her knowledge and experience.

Before giving anything to a person, you should be careful whether he is looking for this kind of help. I have some more thoughts:

- Don't share your knowledge free of cost to a person.

- Give only to those who deserve it.

- Give only to those people who give due respect to "What he received".

- Give only to those who give due respect to the giver.

When knowledge and power are in the hands of the wrong person, then they only create problems for others, and it is the responsibility of the person who gives anything to others, money, knowledge, power, etc. Whether one is competent enough to receive, it is the responsibility of the giver to ensure that it falls into the right hands.

I have experienced that whatever you give to people for free, neither they give their full attention to receive it, nor they give proper respect to the knowledge and the giver also. I learned that people only waste, whatever they get for free.

The rainy season comes after summer when the soil is thirsty and looking for rain in the sky. When it rains, the soil retains every drop of rain and does not waste a single drop. But when the rains come and the soil is not thirsty, the rainwater becomes a quagmire which only creates trouble for the passers-by. Similarly, when a person is not thirsty and gets what he does not deserve, such a person simply wastes what he gets and creates problems for others.

When you give to a person because he is capable of it, he will use all his energy to preserve and expand it. A master has put the seed in the right person's hand and after some time it will become a big tree. But the one who is not worth it only spends his energy on wasted activities. If the seed will not be used properly, it will lose its fertility and after some time will rot and smell.

If a man misuses what he receives, then he will not give any respect to his master. He will only misuse the received knowledge and such activity will cause pain to the master as he has chosen the wrong person who is only causing harm to others. Therefore, it is an obligation for every knowledgeable person to give anything only to the right person and he cannot ignore such an obligation in his life. When a person gives due respect to what he receives, the fragrance of such a flower starts spreading and will soon spread far and wide.

Where there is life there is challenge, and when you overcome the challenges, your soul gets stronger, if you surrender to your greed your soul shrinks, and soon such people are afraid to take any challenge in their life. Life is a journey where every day is not the same and every new situation gives birth to many new paths. So, always choose the right direction in this journey.

3.7 Giving is Freedom, Taking is Bondage

When the clouds are filled with water, they pour water on the earth and make space in the sky, and the empty space is again filled with clouds.

Knowledge is freedom and to get freedom, people are always in search of knowledge. The act of giving provides an opportunity to create more space inside, and as you create the space the invisible hands of nature refill that space. Giving is freedom, a freedom that creates more space, and a space cannot be left empty, it has to be filled quickly and nature fills it soon.

In my corporate career, I have seen that most people are not ready to share anything even with their colleagues and friends, then what to say about sharing and giving to the unknown persons. I have seen that people are so miser that they are not ready to share even few methods in computer with their colleagues. They eat, drink and chat with their colleagues together and know that this man does not know about such methods in computers and will have to sit for hours today to complete the assignment. But they are not ready to share this mere knowledge with their colleagues and expect that soon they will become a highly knowledgeable and respectable person.

Such kind of tactics might work in the organization but nature keeps its records of everything. Later, when their life becomes miserable due to any reason, they expect help from the invisible hands of nature. They were not ready to share even a simple method of computer with their co-worker and they expect someone to come to their aid. The principle of life is that what we give here comes back to us many times over.

In our daily life, our life provides such opportunities to share our knowledge and create space so that nature fills us with more knowledge. But people always show their miserliness and are not ready to give anything. I remember an experience, when I was working in an organization, in the morning I reached the office, I saw one of my colleagues reading the newspaper. I thought it was an official newspaper and when he read it, I asked him to give it to me. He replied, Ajay Ji, this is not an official newspaper, it is my own newspaper which I have bought today. I immediately smiled and said sorry to the person. People are such kind of stingy they cannot share even their newspaper but they expect all kinds of help from others.

Become free from all such shackles and the invisible hands of nature will come to your aid. Give what you can and more will come back to you. Whatever you have given in to the world will come back with multifold and when it returns no one can stop it.

"If you want happiness for an hour, take a nap. If you want happiness for a day, go fishing. If you want happiness for a year, inherit a fortune. If you want happiness for a lifetime, help somebody." - Chinese Proverb

<u>Key Points</u>

- ☞ A courageous and developed soul has the potential to create something in life.

- ☞ Avoid accepting freebies, it will shrink your soul and a shrunken soul cannot do anything constructive in life.

- ☞ When you accept something to satisfy your greed, you will become a timid person.

- ☞ When your life offers an opportunity to expand, don't hold it back, accept it with full courage. Creation is a journey to the unknown that requires a lot of courage.

- ☞ Life is a journey where every day is not the same and every new situation gives birth to many new paths. So, always choose the right direction in this journey.

- ☞ When you have an opportunity to help someone don't miss it, do what you can and more will come back to you.

Chapter 4

The Tree and Its Roots

When you look at a tree, when you take shade under it, when you smell its flowers, when you eat its fruit, when you use its wood, have you ever thought about what source they are coming from. You have to look deep to identify the source that is not visible on the surface. This invisible source not only supports the tree but also helps others through the tree. They are the roots of the tree that are not visible from the surface but the tree cannot stand without them. These roots help the tree in its nutrition and growth. The strength of a tree does not depend on its branches but on its roots. The principle of roots applies to every human being. That is why it has been said that behind every creation there should be strong roots.

4.1 Identify the Roots

Every person must be aware of his roots because it is the roots that give strength in his life. A person who knows where he is from, what type of tradition and culture his roots have been following. Where he stands at present is a point in the long journey of his ancestors and he is also a milestone of this journey on which future generations will come and take recognition to move in the right direction. If he is not aware of his roots then such a person will lack the necessary direction in his life. If he moves in a direction that is not supported by his roots, then all his efforts will go in vain.

Each generation bears all the burden of its previous generation. It is like transferring a chair from one person to another and now it is the obligation of the new person to carry out all the responsibilities. Each new generation gets their physical body from their previous generation. This body carries not only the structure but also the tone, hairstyle, body-color, diseases, etc.

The culture and environment in which this body lives deeply affect it and the person gradually develops into a new individual. This person affected by the new culture and environment cannot run away from his inner creation. He cannot run away from the responsibilities which his previous generation has given and if the person fails to do so then the responsibility falls on his future generations. So, it is the responsibility of every person to fulfill all his obligations and not to transfer any unfulfilled obligation to the forthcoming generations.

Many people think that they love their children by giving them expensive education, clothes, gifts, food, etc. but they forget to teach them to identify their roots and to give them proper respect. They do not know that such an act creates a heavy impact on their children. They are going to increase the burden on their shoulders and with such a heavy burden it will be difficult for them to move ahead in life.

As from the roots tree gets water and all the vital nutrients from the soil and with the help of these roots the tree grows higher. The strength of a tree depends on its roots, because the deeper the roots, the higher the tree is likely to go. The deeper the roots, the taller the tree. If for some reason the root rots or is cut, then the entire strength of the tree disappears and it gradually starts dying. Therefore, to protect the tree, its roots should always be protected. Similarly, when a person is aware of his roots, he uses his energy in the right direction and always moves ahead in his life.

Therefore, it is necessary for every human being to protect his roots and be careful about its proper nurturing and feeding, under any circumstance it does not get rot. Be careful to observe all these activities because you are not separated from your roots, they are they are the basis of your life.

4.2 Stay Connected with Your Roots

The tree exists because of its roots. In the same way, a person exists in this world because someone has taken care of his roots. Now, it is his responsibility to take care of those roots and pass them on to the next generation. It is now his responsibility to stay connected to the roots, and provide them with proper protection, if he fails to do so, along with the death of the tree his time will also be over.

As the tree gets nourishment from its root and grows bigger in the outside world. People come and praise the tree, so suppose sometimes the tree (person) can be arrogant that I have grown so much in the outside world, people come and admire my skill and talent. I have hundreds of branches and thousands of people are taking shelter under me. Why should I worry about these roots that have no identity, why should I stick to these shabby roots, even my connection with them is really hurting me to go higher in the sky? All I want around me is beautiful leaves and branches, where beautiful birds come and sing songs, then the whole atmosphere will become so pleasant, people will admire me that such a person has never been before, and my name and fame will spread far and wide and will be immortal for centuries.

But human life is not as it appears. Whatever is visible in the outside world is not the true picture. The invisible support lies elsewhere and if the tree does not stick to its roots, it will soon wither and die, and no branches, leaves, and birds will come to its rescue.

4.3 Respect Your Roots

The water and nutrition are given to the roots of the tree to keep it alive. Every tree must respect its roots because it is its existence. In the same way, it is necessary for every human being to respect his roots. Today in the modern world we see that young people are hesitant to respect their roots. They only want to respect the beautiful branches, shiny leaves, and singing birds that are visible around them. Therefore, sometimes willingly or unwillingly they forget to give due respect to their roots.

We must remember that respect is the only desirable thing for every human being. If someone starts abusing someone, the other person immediately gets angry because he is asking for respect and he is not getting it in these abusive words. Abusive words do not do any physical harm but these words do not provide proper respect which every human being desires.

Therefore, it is the duty of every person to give due respect to their roots. Because of these roots, he has such a beautiful human body, because of these roots blood is running in his body, because these roots have developed such a sharp brain, which is now praised by everyone.

Any disrespect to the root means that he is disrespecting his existence, and only due to arrogance such kind of activity is possible. The person who is attached to the ground always respects his roots and respect for the roots means its proper nourishment, which means getting proper direction in life which only an experienced person can give because they have seen the different ebb and flow in their life, and the newcomer will see when such time and event passes in their life. It is always necessary to get proper direction for any success in life which a person can get only when he will give proper respect to his roots.

When the environment is good, branches are strong, leaves are shining, birds are singing but if the roots have taken a turn and decided to leave the tree at their own disposal, then such a tree cannot survive for long. From my experience, I can say that this happens only for one reason the tree has not given proper respect to its roots. Till the existing nutrition exists, the tree will take its breath but the death of the tree begins when it stops getting food (necessary direction).

I have seen that when feeding (direction) stops people wander here and there, and with their arrogance and deep pockets, they feel that they can succeed soon. But they forget that every energy (resources) requires direction and without direction, it will go in vain and will disappear after some time. It may be possible that it may take years but when the feeding (direction) will stop, the wandering of the energy starts, and the person will only waste their time.

I have seen that such persons involve themselves in doing various projects, they start one project after some time they start another, and they put a lot of energy into all these activities. But when the guidance gets removed from the life of the person then his futile wandering starts. Soon, the person feels frustrated when the results are not visible. The person has not given due respect to his roots in their life, now the roots have taken a turn and left the tree in its condition.

It doesn't take time to cut or destroy anything, but it takes a lot of time to heal that. Be careful what you are going to cut or destroy because you are not aware of how much time it will take to heal and sometimes it becomes impossible to recover.

4.4 You Are Not Isolated

A person who is connected with their roots and gives them proper respect can never take any wrong step in his life. Now he has a meaningful purpose in his life, he knows the reason for these strong branches, shining leaves, and singing birds, he knows the reason for their existence. He never gets disappointed in his life when his life cycle takes a U-turn. He is not a useless person who wastes his time only on bad habits. He is not the kind of person who wastes whatever he got from his previous generation. He has full responsibility to fulfill his obligations and transfer it to the next generation.

He is not an isolated person in this world because his roots are strong, and he is doing every effort to make them stronger. These invisible roots are the strength and with such strong strength he can overcome any obstacle in this world. Anything you do to strengthen your roots are actually strengthening yourselves. A person who is connected with roots is ready to walk in the unknown world of creation as he is not afraid of the challenges that come his way.

"Someone's sitting in the shade today because someone planted a tree a long time ago." – Warren Buffett

<u>Key Points</u>

- Behind every creation there must be strong roots.

- One must always stay connected with their roots; it is the roots that give the strength in one's life.

- When a person is aware of his roots, he uses his energy in the right direction and always moves ahead in his life.

- It is necessary for every human being to respect his roots.

- It doesn't take time to cut anything, but it takes a lot of time for healing, be careful what you are going to cut because you are not aware of the time of healing.

- A person who is connected with his roots is not an isolated person in this world.

Chapter 5

Time and Energy

Time is eternal and every present moment changes into the past that never comes back. Physicists define 'Time' as the progression of events from the past to the present into the future. Along with the three spatial dimensions, time is called the fourth dimension.

In physics, energy is the quantitative property that is transferred to a body or to a physical system, recognizable in the performance of work and in the form of heat and light. Energy is a conserved quantity; the law of conservation of energy states that energy can be converted in form, but not created or destroyed.

Human life passes through different stages and in every stage its energy level is different. Among them, adolescence and early adulthood age are very important. This is the time when the energy level in the human body is getting high. Before adolescence, children are dependent on their parents for everything, but after the age of 12, the energy level in the body is getting high and biological changes start in their body and reflect in various emotional, sexual, and cultural passions. Therefore, an adolescent should not waste this energy on worthless matters because this is the time to create a strong foundation for his life. Energy always requires direction without direction it will go in vain. Every adolescent must follow his passion to learn new skills, read good books, learn whatever he wants to do in his life further, and put all his energy in that direction. They should set a goal for their life and start building a foundation to achieve that goal in the later years of their life.

This is the time of development and every development requires a strong foundation. Energy brings enthusiasm and this is the time to make strong pillars for his life. So, a teenager should not waste such creative energy on useless matters.

My father once shared an experience from his life. When he was young and doing graduation, he used to spend his time in the college library. At that time, he had read a book and the knowledge of that book helped him at the age of 62. In the meantime, he had completely forgotten about the name of the book and what he had read, but when the need arose, his mind immediately remembered it. He told me that whatever you read and learn once, gets stored in your mind, and it opens up when you need it.

5.1 Adolescence and Early Adulthood Age

This is the golden age of the human body. The energy level is high, the level of enthusiasm is high, the passion is high, the courage and the risk-taking ability are high, and the adventurous ability is also high. Adolescence is the age when a person sows the seeds for his future. Whatever seed he will sow during this time, will germinate when it meets with a suitable environment. When there is no seed, no matter how much energy you put into the later stage of life, there will be no germination and therefore no fruit.

We see that nowadays it is difficult for old age people to operate mobile phones and other latest technological gadgets, but kids learn quickly. This is their time to learn and nature supports them to learn quickly. Therefore, adolescents should not waste their valuable time in worthless wandering here and there, gossiping and discussing worthless movies and television serials. By getting involved in these kinds of acts, such adolescents only waste their valuable time, because they will not get such kind of energy again in life.

Later, whatever they want to do, any new creation, starting any new enterprise, it would be very difficult for them, because they cannot face the adversity that comes while walking on a new path. When some obstacle comes, they feel disappointed and soon they leave the path forever. When there was time to learn how to fight against the odds, they wasted their time and energy on worthless gossiping, now this energy will not get again in their life.

After adolescence, the age of 21 to 28 is again a very important stage in a person's life. Along with the higher energy level, one starts getting direction in his life. What does he want to do in his life, and which field does he like the most for his career?

When the energy gets a proper direction then the wandering stops and one uses all his energy in one direction only to get maximum results. It is like fixing the flame of a burner at a point in one direction, when it reaches an optimum level, the maximum result is achieved.

This is the time when a person should use the energy for his development. It is good to collect more knowledge and develop more skills because it may be difficult in later stages of your life. Like an old person finds it difficult to learn to operate a mobile, natural energy does not support learning a new skill at the later stage of your life, you have to work hard to learn anything new. So, any creation will be very difficult if you have not sown its seed before.

5.2 Sexual Energy

Sexual energy is the most powerful energy in the human body. This energy has given birth to us. Physical changes start when a child reaches adolescence age. Adolescence is the time to preserve this energy, always be careful and should not waste it under any circumstances. If an adolescent indulges in sexual activity, he will miss such a great chance to utilize such powerful energy in a constructive manner. Indulgence in sexual activity will also hamper the development of his mind. He will lose courage and the ability to speak when needed. Such a person will not get a sharp mind in his life, he will remain a person of a very mediocre mind and will never be able to become an intelligent and wise person.

The ancient Hindu texts divide human life into four stages and till the age of 25 is known as brahmacharya. The ancient texts say that one must follow the path of brahmacharya (Celibacy) till the age of 25. If a person follows the path of celibacy till the age of 25 then his mind will develop and he will become a sharp-minded person. Only the person whose brain is developed can do something constructive in his life.

"Power comes to him who observes unbroken Brahmacharya for a period of twelve years. Complete continence gives great intellectual and spiritual power. Controlled desire leads to the highest results. Transform the sexual energy into spiritual energy. The stronger this force, the more can be done with it. Only a powerful current of water can do hydraulic mining." - Swami Vivekananda

5.3 Control Your Energy

When a person wants to do something constructive in his life, when a person wants to attain some desired goal, when a person wants to develop a new skill in his life, all these acts require energy and only focused energy can do something constructive in life. Therefore, a person has to control his energy from various aspects and put it only in one direction, then the energy starts giving its maximum results.

A person starts fighting on the road, starts abusing others, spent hours in worthless discussions and playing cards because he doesn't know what to do with this time. Such person does not have any desire to develop a new skill, such types of people do not have any goals in their life. Every goal requires your attention. If you want to clear an exam it requires your attention and continued effort. If you want to learn new software, if you want to develop a new skill, anything you want to do constructively in your life requires your attention.

Without giving proper attention and stopping the wastage of energy, it is difficult to rise high in life.

It is always easy to go down in life but it is always difficult to go up. It requires your energy and energy needs direction. Energy will produce its maximum results when it is completely controlled and focused on only one direction. When a person controls his energy on worthless matters and pours it into a single direction, such energy automatically uplifts the person. Remember the definition of energy written above, "*...... energy can be converted in form, but not created or destroyed*".

5.4 Choose Your Steps Carefully

There are many choices that come in our life but at a time we have to choose only one and whatever we choose we make a relationship with them and after that, we are responsible for all the pros and cons related to it. The time of adolescence and early adulthood is very important because it is the time every person is creating their pillars which will help them further to build a strong building in their life.

As I have written above, this is the time for teenagers to develop their hobbies and skills and choose their career paths carefully which require a lot of focus and hard work. At a time, out of the various available options, a person has to choose only one and cannot undo whatever he chooses as time goes by. Whatever you choose, you have created a pillar for your future.

For example, suppose one evening a person has options to watch a movie or gossip with friends or go to a party, or develop his skills. He can only do one thing at a time and whatever he chooses will form a pillar for his future. Material success or failure is a different matter but the learning capacity at this time is very high and whatever a person learns at this stage will never go in vain.

At that time, I (the author of the book) could not succeed in those fields in which I wanted to be successful, but all that knowledge is now contributing to the writing of my books.

5.5 Try to Keep Balance in Life

When people start running after their desires, they start crossing their limits. When energy is focused its strength is high, its power to penetrate the object also becomes high, and then a person can easily achieve their desired object. But remember all these energies are coming from your body and every human body has its own capacity. If one day you put more energy than your regular energy then the next day your body demands rest, and if you are not able to take proper rest then you are prone to diseases.

If you put extra energy from your eyes; very soon you will have to put on glasses, now doctors advise you that take a rest in between your work. If you are a workaholic, without papers you cannot sit then the day will come when the opposite of this will become true. One day you will have to sit in a hospital room without papers. I have seen that sometimes such kind of workaholic people take a rest much longer than expected in a room, all their haste disappears. If you are creating an imbalance with your own body, then one-day nature will balance it.

Day and night are equally balanced; the day is beautiful but it does not mean that night has less importance than a day. Everything is balanced in nature, and where there is an imbalance, natural forces immediately run to fill the gap but then strong winds and storms create. Wikipedia states, "A storm is any disturbed state of an environment or in an astronomical body's atmosphere especially affecting its surface, and strongly implying severe weather. It may be marked by significant disruptions to normal conditions."

The same thing happens to human life also. If you create imbalance by your act, then someday your life will create such circumstances that will force you to maintain balance. A person who is running behind the money day and night, and leaves everything in his life, then one day their life will force them to sit in a place either at the home, hospital or in a prison.

Whatever the imbalance the person has created so far, the natural forces will fill the gap either by way of high winds or storms and the person will have to face these changed winds in his life.

The capacity of our mind is infinite but the capacity of our body is limited, there must be a proper synchronization between these two while performing any act, when a person fails to do so, then he starts creating a gap. As the gap widens, the person is unknowingly opening the way for the storm in his life. When a person turned the pleasant breeze of his life into a storm, he might not know, but he will have to face all the consequences because this gap is created by his actions. When the wind turns, natural forces will rush to fill the gap in his life. So, it is better to maintain balance in every matter of life otherwise nature will do it in its own way because humans are part of nature.

5.6 High Wave Principle

When a person stops wasting his energy on useless gossip, street fighting, watching worthless television serials, etc. and starts focusing it in one direction then that energy gradually starts accumulating. It is like a tidal wave where it is scattered at the bottom, but when it gets a direction, it starts to accumulate and as it accumulates it starts rising upwards. Upward movement takes time and it varies for each wave. Hence, a person should not look for success immediately, after putting in some effort. Many people without preparing the proper base, start getting feelings of frustration only after putting in some energy when their desired outcome is not reflected.

When the energy is high and its direction is clear then the wave starts moving upwards and one day such a wave will hit the rock (desired object) which is present on the top of the mountain, which seemed impossible to hit when the wave has started its accumulation work. No matter how far the rock is situated on the top of the mountain and how much time the wave will take to hit that rock, once the accumulation starts and the direction is clear, surely it will hit (achieve) one day.

The principle of High Wave works behind every achievement and every creation. When a person starts accumulating his energy, every drop count. One cannot say that a drop is worthless, to fulfill such a task requires a huge amount of energy, and reaching the rock is impossible with such a tiny drop.

There is a story in Ramayana, Lord Rama needed to build a bridge across the sea to Lanka, the army started building the bridge with rocks and heavy stones. A squirrel also collected small pebbles and small bits of sand and started contributing to building the bridge. A monkey asked what he was doing there, the squirrel replied that it was carrying pebbles and sand to build the bridge. Then the monkey laughed that such a bridge requires great effort and big resources and, therefore, you should get out of the way.

Then Lord Rama picked up the little squirrel, thanked him for all his hard work, and said, "*Always remember, however small, every task is equally important. A project can never be completed by the main people alone. It requires everyone's support, and no matter how small the support is, an effort should always be appreciated.*"

Key Points

- Energy always requires direction without direction it will go in vain.

- Seed is necessary for germination. Adolescence is the age when a person sows the seeds for his future.

- For any achievement it is necessary to control the wastage of energy on useless things and make it flow in one direction.

- Do not distract yourself by charms and choose your options carefully, your choices are the pillars of your future.

- Try to keep balance in every aspect of your life.

- Every tiny drop counts for the achievement of a goal.

Chapter 6

Key Pillars
For Creation

"Each work has to pass through these stages – ridicule, opposition, and then acceptance. Those who think ahead of their time are sure to be misunderstood". – Swami Vivekananda

A strong foundation is necessary to do something constructive in life. Without a foundation, if a person starts working on walls and ceilings just to show off then that construction cannot last long, such is good only to take photographs and for showy purposes. While walking on the path of creation it is necessary to create strong pillars which will help you to achieve the objective.

6.1 Thirst for Creation

On this path, a high level of positive energy is required that pushes you to do constructive work in your life. Travelling on such a path is a long journey and many times your mind will say to go back, why you are taking unnecessary risk that no one has taken. It is better to go back and live a peaceful life. But something is there in the person's soul which cannot let him sleep and that is called "Thirst". A person who is thirsty cannot go back on the chosen path in his life, despite various obstacles.

A person who is not satisfied with his present existence and is looking for something else in his life is really a thirsty person. To move ahead in life, to do something constructive in life, such a thrust is necessary. A person who is not thirsty will take no interest in any type of learning and development. He will not take any risk because an unknown path is always risky and you cannot sleep where there is danger. While travelling on such a path his mind will be activated and this kind of activity will help him to make a foundation that will lead him on the path to success. (Readers can refer to my book "Psychology And Investment" to read more about this topic.)

6.2 Go It Alone

When you decide to do something constructive in your life, sometimes you start to feel that people are not taking any interest in the direction you have chosen. The path may be known or unknown but the fact is that people will discuss with you only your aspirations and plans but will not give you any support. They will promise to help you but won't help you, because they want to keep you on the same level. This kind of behaviour sometimes surprise you, maybe you never expected it, but the truth in this world is that you have to go it alone in your chosen direction.

A person who wants to do something creative in his life should have enough courage to walk on his path alone. If he says that I will move when I get support, then he will go nowhere. Such a statement is showing that he is afraid of being alone and of the possible obstacles he may face in the future. People with such lukewarm tendencies give up soon and start blaming others for not supporting him. Have the courage to walk your own path alone, you'll be surprised how soon new dimensions begin to form.

The path of creation needs a person who has enough courage to go it alone, a person who is not afraid of circumstances, a person who does not look for support for every trivial problem in life, a person who makes decisions and stands firm on that and says whether right or wrong, I am the responsible person. Decide in your mind, have faith in God, and start moving forward, soon the pillars would begin to form, and each small construction would pave the way for a stronger building.

"If they answer not to thy call walk alone"
- Rabindranath Tagore

6.3 Be a Humble Person

Life is a long journey and a person who wants to do something concrete in his life has to leave his arrogance. A person's arrogance is like a thorn who pinches his nearby surroundings. Soon, people try to avoid such kind of person because his every act pinch thorn to others. When people have any compulsion to work with such kind of person, then knowingly or unknowingly, they develop their shields and when an arrogant person throws thorns, they put their shield in front of him.

This shield can be of any kind but a clever man knows how to deal with an egotistical person. In my corporate career, I have seen clever employees quickly develop their shield with their haughty bosses, but their whole energy is involved in strengthening their shield. Like, they willingly delay the work and put it forward when the time is favourable. When a team of such type is involved in a big project, not only does work get delayed but there are other negative consequences.

"If you build an army of 100 lions and their leader is a dog, in any fight, the lions will die like a dog. But if you build an army of 100 dogs and their leader is a lion, all dogs will fight like a lion." – Napoleon Bonaparte

Humbleness is the foremost criterion to do anything constructive in life. A person cannot do anything creative if he is full of ego, and ego means such a person stops his development. He is overloaded with that and stops looking for anything new in his life. A person who is full of ego always looks downward and never looks upward, otherwise in this vast universe what is the meaning of such a frivolous ego.

Look at the sky at night, and enjoy the brightness of the moon and stars. Start giving thanks to "The Creator of All" and feel lucky for getting such a chance in human life. Then there is no point in such petty arrogance and putting thorns in the lives of others. Become a humble person and now your eyes start looking upward in the sky. Now you start elevating yourself to the next level of development. Now you started your journey on the path of creation.

"Humility is the solid foundation of all virtues."
- Confucius

6.4 Praise Others

People hesitate to praise others; they feel jealous when their friends or colleagues get successful. Very unwillingly they praise, clap, and smile at someone else achievements. Children are jealous of each other but when a grown-up person feels jealous it is a sign that child-level jealousy still exists in their mind.

People feel that when they praise others, when they clap for others, then another person will be benefitted and what he will achieve while doing such activity. I have seen that when a person is very happy or has to show happiness by any compulsion, he beats the table two or three times and that is enough for him, he has shown his happiness, even he is not even ready to give his clap to others.

People are so miser; they think that their praising and clapping activity will be beneficial for others and in return what they will achieve. They are always ready to abuse others in any matter and they feel very pleasure in doing such activity that they have thrown some thorn in other's life. After doing such kind of mischievous act they feel that their life is secure and now others will feel the pain of these thorns.

But human life is not as simple as it appears on the surface. Abuse is never given to anyone else and clap is never played for anyone else. A person gives all the abuses to himself and all the applause he plays for himself. An abuse always leaves a scar on your soul. A person who uses abusive words gradually develops various negative traits in his personality.

Gradually, such a person will lose courage and always thinks about taking a back foot on every matter in life. He will always be afraid of the unknown fear and hesitate to go alone on unknown paths. He may think that he has given a scar to others but in reality, his every action has wounded his own soul.

When you praise others, your heart widens, if you praise selflessly, you feel joy from within. Use a method, try admiring the plants, flowers, sunrise, and beautiful nature in your surroundings for a month and you will not be the same person. A kind-hearted person never envies the success of others. Once you taste the joy and now the secret is in your hands. Your every act to praise others selflessly is your preparation to go on the path of creation.

Praise your friends and colleagues for every small success and if you are unable to give anything at least you can give them a beautiful smile, give them a clap wholeheartedly and remember these claps are not for others, you are playing it for yourself, the others are just a medium. Whenever you get a chance to clap, utilize it with full potential, and do not beat the tables, all these are worthless activities, you will not get any benefit from doing that.

The science of acupressure says that there are about 30+ acupressure points in the palms, which are activated when a person clap. These points have direct connections to different organs of the body, clapping is known to improve overall heart health and improve blood pressure. Blood circulation to various organs is also improved by regular clapping.

The person who admires others opens the door to enhance his creative abilities. Every act of praising others counts and this increases positive energy, with such positive energy a person never feels disappointed in life. Against all odds, he is highly motivated and his journey towards the achievement of his greatest creation continues.

6.5 Choose Your Relationships Carefully

When you are moving in some direction then your thoughts will not match with those who are going in another direction or who are not moving anywhere in their life. Every direction has its own importance and a person moving in any other direction cannot walk along with you. In such situations, you have to choose your relationships carefully because maybe someone else's life direction is completely different, so sometimes you may have the option to choose either the relationship with the person or the direction. Life is not static, it goes on every day and if you are in the right direction many others will start following the same path.

Many people do not have the courage to take initiative and they require some push to move forward. Therefore, when you are heading in a direction choose your relationship carefully. Your judgment should be right and the person should take an interest to go in your direction. For those whose life-energy does not match with yours they cannot go longer and if such energy does not support you then due to such kind of disharmony in relationships you find yourself in a state of complete disarray and such type of situation creates unnecessary trouble in your life.

6.6 Do Not Run from Problems

Problems are part of the journey. They will come when you move in any direction. Life is easy when you will sit in one place and go nowhere, but it also means that no vitality is there and also no life is there. People always complain about problems in life, but problems are an integral part of life. Once you face a challenge and overcome that it strengthens your personality. A person who has not faced any challenge in life is actually a dud person.

Life is a journey of many ups and downs, and no situation in life remains the same and no situation in life lasts forever. Up means, a downward cycle is waiting, and down means, an upward journey is about to begin. Time never remains the same nor waits for anyone, life goes on like a wheel.

When we confront a challenge, our brain gets activated and those cells of our brain that we have never used before, start working. When we are more focused, the entire brain cells are engaged in finding solutions. When I am looking for a solution I adopt a technique, I study all the necessary information deeply, think deeply and keep all the available information in my mind, and think about various scenarios.

When my mind is tense, I leave it for few hours and stop thinking about the problem, then suddenly any time while walking down the street or sipping a cup of tea, I find my solution. This happens because our brain cells have worked hard to find the solution and they have found it but it doesn't come out on the surface because of the stressed nerves. Our brain recalls it when the nerves get relaxed. But the first exercise is necessary otherwise our mind will not work and the solution will not come to our mind.

People get discouraged when they realize that despite all their hard work, they aren't seeing any results. They have high hopes, but when difficulties arise, they start to lose confidence. Even a small problem seems insurmountable when they don't see any progress after putting in some effort. Instead of trying to solve the problem, they prefer to waste their time watching pointless television shows and gossiping.

They begin to believe that it's an endless process and will yield no results, so it's better to give up; that's the safest thing they can do. Such people don't want to spend time laying the foundation for creation. Everyone is eager to enjoy the fruits, even if it means snatching them from others and compromising their integrity, but no one wants to plant a tree and wait for it to bear fruit. A person who lacks patience cannot give birth to any creativity.

But you move in any direction, problems are waiting for you. There is no red-carpet welcome on any path which first time you are travelling upon. When you are accustomed to the path then you can sing a song, but at first, you have to clear all the pebbles and stones on those paths on which you are not known. Some stones are small and some are big ones that take time to remove, but remember that there is no such stone on the road, which will stop a traveler's way forever.

Avoid going into self-pity mode and do not discuss your problem with everyone. Self-pity mode stops your mind to think in an accurate manner, and your discussion with others is only a waste of time and energy. There are a lot of negative and noxious people out there, they discourage you and like to hamper your chosen path.

Discuss only with people of your same mindset. Discuss only who takes a real interest. Now, how do we know whether a person will take real interest or not? My experience is that, if a person discusses from which source the problem is coming or what is the root of the problem then he will take an interest and if he wants to know only what is the benefit over about and what benefit he will get and what benefit you will get then he will not take any interest. The real truth is that people will not support you and when you discuss your problem, rather they feel pleasure inside.

Face the problem with full courage. Apply your brain which is capable enough to provide you with a solution, the problem is that you have never demanded that solution.

In fact, problems are demanding your attention, so don't blame anyone. It is providing you a chance, a chance to exercise your mind, so be alert and face it with full courage. Sometimes, you will find that once you decided to face the problem and the problem disappears. It is like it was never there, it was only your hallucination. Only this thought to face the problem has changed you and you raise one step ahead on your path. Now you have become a courageous person who can face more severe problems, running from a problem will make you a timid person.

If you run away from an obstacle, it doesn't mean that the obstacle has gone out of the way, it will be there for you and waiting for you to come and remove it. Anytime when you return to the journey, you will have to start from there. It doesn't matter how many years have passed but it will be there for you. Running away from the situation will always be in your memories, you discouraged your own soul because you cannot run away from yourself. Time is providing you an opportunity to turn stones into stairs and go ahead.

The person who faces problems and seeks solutions always has an active mind. Once you understand how to deal with them, then you have become like an expert driver, whose car can cross any obstacle on the road. Now it is not going to stop, because the driver had not stopped learning to drive and if he had given up, he would never have learned to drive. Problems are the same as only those who struggle, they succeed and take the life on a long path with different experiences.

Running away from a problem does not mean fixing it. Fight until you win, and enjoy the joy of success in your life, which you can enjoy only if you have not given up on it.

"When you don't come across any problem, you can be sure that you are travelling in a wrong train." - Swami Vivekananda

6.7 Stop Passing Worthless Information

People who want to do something concrete in life must stop passing the information of one person to another person. Knowingly or unknowingly people transfer what they listen to from one person to another person. This type of attitude reduces their constructive thinking because anything constructive always begins at the deepest point when everything is silent and totally isolated from the activities of the outer world.

The person who wants to do something constructive and engages himself, such person does not have time to transfer any worthless information to another person. Most people transfer only trivial information about their day-to-day life. Moreover, they are interested in saying rather than listening and the other person is waiting for when you stop and he starts speaking and pouring all the worthless information into your mind. When they pour out information into others' minds then they say that the meeting was very fruitful but other than pouring the trivial information nothing else they transferred. These types of activities are useless and if you engage yourself in these activities then you miss out on your vital focus which is essential for any positive activity.

6.8 Think for the Long Term

When one thinks about the long term, the first question that comes up is whether the long-term strategy works or not, who has seen the future after 5 years or 10 years. Capitalize on what you have on your hand right now and don't waste time and energy making long-term plans. There is no certainty about the long term and you can lose even short-term gains. Many people spend their lives on this short-term profit policy. Thinking about short-term gains all the time gradually narrows their eyesight and they do not have the ability to see the opportunity that is knocking at the door, as long-term gains take time to materialize.

Once one of my seniors Mr. Utpal Choudhury shared his experience with me. He told me when he was in a city and needed a different kind of pen. He went to a stationery shop and asked to show such a pen. The shop owner said that he does not have that kind of pen but he has other type of pen which can be better than what you are demanding. Then he said 'OK' show me the pen. The shop owner thinks for a while and says, "I will not show you, because your gesture is telling me that you are not going to buy it, showing you the pen is a waste of time". He was surprised by such an answer.

That's what most people think, they are only interested in short-term gains, which are clearly visible before the eyes. The shop-owner is not looking for the opportunity which he got to sell another pen, although after seeing the customer may purchase it or not. But this is the opportunity that demands some exercise and as far as the shopkeeper is concerned, he thinks that his exercise will be in vain as there is no immediate profit in it.

This is the thinking of most people that they take an interest only in short-term gains that is clearly visible in front of their eyes. They do not bother to think about the long term. They want easy and quick money in their hand, right now and here. Such type of people lacks the quality of patience in their life.

But every creation takes time and requires patience. Whether you want to master a skill, you want to build a business, or anything that puts you ahead of others, it requires long-term planning. **Whatever hard work you do will never go in vain, however, it may not be cashed in immediately, but it counts in your efforts and these small efforts make pillars for a bigger achievement.**

The visionary always thinks for the long term. His eyes are always looking for an opportunity that does not currently exist but he is seeing that it is coming gradually and he is ready to wait for it. Patience is one of the most desirable qualities for a person who is looking for big gains. If you are not ready to wait for something, then you cannot see things that are not present now but will become visible after some time.

Try to learn patience in every small matter of life, don't lose your temper quickly. As you learn patience in your life, you can see that what doesn't exist yet but is ready to come, all you have to do is make way for it. Then you engage yourself in the creation of your purpose because you know it will take time but one day it will become a reality.

"Successful Investing takes time, discipline and patience. No matter how great the talent or effort, some things just take time: You can't produce a baby in one month by getting nine women pregnant." - Warren Buffett

6.9 Avoid Flatterers & Sycophants

When people around you say how smart you are, how beautifully you deal with a situation that no one can, you know that these are all false but hearing these words makes the person feel better. When you are in a powerful position, sycophants, advisors, and subordinates know that their job is only to praise your decision. The senior person thinks that these people are loyal to me, but in reality they are deceitful, they are only loyal to their greed.

Flatterers & sycophants are cowards. Every act of flattery loosens the courage of the person and gradually he becomes a timid person. The act of flattery gives birth to procrastination. The person is ready to do anything that their bosses said, but unwilling to do any act said by others. Gradually, the person becomes a lethargic person, because his mind works only on the voice of their bosses. He is not taking any other work from the rest of his mind. Therefore, such kind of person is giving birth to inertia in his personality.

The flatterers and sycophants have only one aim, they want something from you and for that, they are ready to do anything because refusal can be dangerous. The person in power and position may get angry and the greed of flatterers and sycophants may come in trouble.

Hence, they always say "Yes sir". They always praise their bosses on each decision taken by them. Their motto is "The boss is always right", because boss has the power to give them promotion, money, etc., and the flatterers and sycophants are not fools who put all of these in jeopardy. By saying lush words, actually, they are demanding from their bosses but their demand is hidden in their sycophancy.

They are deceivers, currently, they are deceiving their bosses for their personal gains. They deceive the person with their juicy words which makes a person feel good. The characteristic of flatterers is that they wait for their time to speak and they always speak in a very smooth manner. They always represent only those points which their bosses are ready to agree. They say only what their bosses want to listen and almost every person likes their admiration and the truth hurts. Saying to your boss that your strategy has failed is risky, therefore, flatterers always say that boss you are a genius, and silently say give me the promotion, money, etc. But their bosses listen only to the first part of the sentence and feel very happy, that is the reason, licking the soles works in the organization. In my corporate career, I noticed some of the characteristics of these flatterers;

- Without completion of their boss sentences, they are ready to say "Yes Sir".

- When meeting in a group they always praise their bosses in front of others.

- Their focus is less on their responsibilities and more on their bosses.

- They are not working for the organization; they are working for their bosses and ready to do any job told by them.

- They always use very mild words in front of their bosses but their behaviour is totally opposite in front of others. They become very arrogant and use very harsh and abusive words towards their colleagues and subordinates.

The person who licks the soles because of his greed lowers his self-esteem and puts his greed ahead. But every soul wants respect, so licking or flattering hurts the 'Soul' of flatterers and sycophants also. But greed is more important, so they bury that wound at that time, but every hidden wound slowly turns into a canker and takes its full revenge when the time comes.

The person who is pressing the feet today is actually waiting for the time to press the neck of their boss. But the neck is far away, he cannot catch it straight, so he started with the feet. A flatterer is filling the boss's ego and clearing their path to go ahead, and ego is more important for the bosses that is the reason flattery works. However, the boss doesn't know but he is providing the flatterers a chance to come close to his neck.

Be careful about all those flatterers and sycophants. Every rise of these kinds of people is actually providing them a chance to catch your neck, and one day they will catch it, then they will take full revenge for all their hidden wounds from all those people because they are bearing those wounds for a long time.

6.10 Avoid Temptation

As you move towards your destination there are many temptations that want to deviate you from your path and tell you to accept such things and surrender yourself. They say look at those who are enjoying, then why are you causing unnecessary trouble. But remember this is your journey, which you can complete only with your courage. When you come across any temptation think for a while;

- Where was this temptation when you were thinking of embarking on the journey?

- Where was such temptation when you had taken the first step with full alertness?

Those who are tempting you are not aware of your courage. Now temptation is coming to you because you have crossed a milestone. Many people don't have the vision to see beyond the curtains, they can only see what is apparent, and now your milestone is visible. With a little bit of courage, you have crossed such a milestone, so don't give up and don't succumb to your temptation. the path of creation is a long journey in which you have to cross many milestones.

Key Points

- A soul which is thirsty cannot go back against all odds in his life.

- Be a humble person and don't put thorns in the lives of others.

- Praise your friends and colleagues and clap for them wholeheartedly, remember these claps are not for others, you are giving them to yourself.

- Don't run from problems, they are part of the journey. Show your courage and face it, they will disappear like never before.

- Running away from a problem does not mean fixing it. Fight till you win, and enjoy the joy of success, which you can enjoy only if you have not given up on it.

- Be careful of flatterers and sycophants and avoid them always. They are cowardly and deceitful people.

- Avoid any kind of temptation, there is a long journey you have to complete.

Chapter 7

Attention and Nurturing

"Do not give your attention to what others do or fail to do; give it to what you do or fail to do." – Lord Buddha

One needs to be reasonably attentive before entering the path of creation. It is one of the most essential skills that a person must possess otherwise he may fall from the chosen path. Utmost care should be taken while doing work. One must pay attention to every detail otherwise even an act of carelessness and a big mistake may be possible.

7.1 Attention

When you pay attention to your work the whole cell of your mind awakens and under this awakening, it is difficult for others to deceive you. People are ready to make you a fool and they want to enjoy your foolishness. They are waiting for the moment to take advantage, when you fall asleep and make a mistake. I have seen in my corporate career that people are ready to take any advantage of you, if you make any mistake, they are ready to take leverage on yours even if they are eating with you, laughing with you, and claiming to be a close friend.

One should always be attentive and not be supposed to do any mistakes related to your work. People are waiting for the moment to take advantage of others' foolishness. Therefore, it is your duty to be attentive to every moment at any cost, without such a quality you cannot proceed on the path of creation which is completely unknown to you. The unknown is always risky and only your observant nature can lead you on such a path. When you are attentive then your brain gets the job of alertness and under such alertness, one can easily identify wrong steps and stop himself from going ahead.

When a person is moving toward the path of the unknown every single decision is important and it should be taken with full alertness because these decisions prepare the path on which your further activities will progress. Therefore, every such decision should be taken with utmost care. In case of mistakes, you should not do it again, experience is the greatest teacher and everyone learns from his own experience.

A person who always keeps himself in a sleep zone is more likely to repeat the same mistake time and again in his life. This type of person talks only of his great plan but they are always afraid to pursue it. Because, they have not developed the quality of alertness in their mind, therefore, they are always afraid of taking independent decisions and want to follow only those paths which are already followed by many. In this way, they want to keep their mind in the sleep zone and feel great pleasure over the mistakes of others.

For a person who has taken the courage to go on the path to create something, mistakes are likely to be possible but do not repeat the same. On this path, you have to walk alone because;

- There are no signboards here

- No one is here who can provide some help

- No one is here with whom you can discuss when you face any problem

- No one is here who extends his hand when you are looking for some rescue

This is the path of risk, this is the path to the unknown, and this is the path to creation, which you can win only when you have the quality of alertness in your personality. (Readers can refer to my book "Psychology And Investment" to know more about alertness.)

7.2 Nurturing

Once you have decided to proceed with your decision, every step of yours is important. Your every decision on this path is contributing something and based on that you can take big decisions later. Therefore, it is very important to nurture each stage. You are responsible for all the outcomes because you have given birth to such outcomes and now it is your baby. Now you have to provide proper protection for it, and you should take care of its proper nurturing.

Many people make mistakes like after taking a few steps they start beating their small trumpet here and there. Beating the trumpet represents that they are satisfied with such steps and they start wasting their energy in such discussions. They feel that with whom they are discussing are their well-wishers but others are waiting to catch it. They are waiting for the moment when you will go into the sleep zone and they will kick you off.

Just as parents protect their children, every step on this path and its consequences is your responsibility. Now it is your duty to protect it from the outside world and provide the proper nurturing. Take care of all your results, do not beat the trumpet of your small success here and there, and silently get involved in the completion of the task.

Remember the day you first decided to go alone, remember the day you took your first decision on these unknown paths, remember how much attention you have paid when everything was unknown. After investing so much time and energy now you have something in your hand, but if you are not able to digest it from the outside world then your small mistake will destroy it all.

With your courage you have reached here, so do not be afraid of moving forward. Remember, only a few people in the world have the courage enough to go ahead on the path of the unknown. Many people keep themselves in their protected zone and don't want to come out of their shells. Your one such step on these unknown paths keeps you separate from many people. One such step on this path will completely change your personality and soon you will find that you have become a different kind of person from those shell-seeking people.

The path of creation is such a path once you have taken a step it will completely change your life. This path is not for those who are always looking for safe steps in their life. The journey on this path requires courage and quality of alertness, with these qualities you can clear all the hurdles coming on the path, and every clearance of these hurdles will increase your confidence to move forward.

<u>Key Points</u>

- Before entering the path of the unknown a person must possess the quality of attention in his personality.

- Take care of all your results, do not beat the trumpet of your small success here and there otherwise people are ready to kick you off.

- The path of creation is such a path once you have taken a step it will completely change your life.

Chapter 8

Imagination and Success

"The true sign of intelligence is not knowledge but imagination." - Albert Einstein

Imagination is a very powerful technique to accomplish whatever you want to achieve in your life. Every creation begins with imagination and it is not concerned with daydreaming and illusion. When a person imagines something deeply, then his mind is not unstable as that of a confused person, because such energy of imagination is coming from his soul. Such energy does not allow a person to sit idle like a daydreamer who discusses a lot and makes no effort to achieve the task and always blames the lack of time to put in some effort.

A clear image of your plan helps you take your steps carefully and takes decisive action. Strong planning always starts with good imagination that further converts into a strategy and later completion of the task. If a person fails to manage his daily assignment, then it is not possible for him to proceed with a deep image that requires a lot of energy.

A strong imagination does not allow a person to sit silently in one place even if the person is living in a room, and has only one chair to sit on, but his mind constantly works on what to do towards the accomplishment of the objective. The precision of thinking develops with the power of imagination that leads the person to make the right decisions when a critical situation arises. When a person starts on a path without imagination, the work gets delayed due to poor planning and the chances of failure are high due to lack of direction.

8.1 Power of Imagination

The power of imagination is very strong and such energy compels a person to move ahead in life and convert imagination into reality. Without a strong imagination, it is difficult for a person to achieve what he wants in his life. With such a strong imagination, our mind becomes active and then its visuals remain no longer dreams. It may be a dream for others but every step taken on that path is gradually turning it into reality. At this stage, only those who can see beyond the curtains can see such transformation.

Such strong imagination drives the person to move forward and the energy of your mind starts capturing the vibrations from the environment. With such energy, your brain will work only with those people who want to come on this path and will take interest in turning it into a reality.

Imagination is a very powerful technique for creation and success. It is not limited to certain achievements or fulfilment of some mundane desires. Whatever you imagine in your mind and put your energy into it, one day it will become a reality.

8.2 Your Imagination is the Seed

The first seed of creation, achievement, and success comes to our minds through imagination. Your imagination is such a seed that has enormous potential to become a big tree. Feel lucky when such an image comes into your mind because there are many people in the world who never think of doing anything creative in their life. Nature has given you such a seed because you are the one who has the potential to convert it into a tree. Now it is your duty to plant such seeds, provide proper nutrition, and provide protection from outside, so that one day it will grow and provide shelter to others.

8.3 Imagination and Transformation

The transformation of a person begins when he thinks about his imagination and forces his energy to move in that direction. This image in your mind will change your life completely, so it is necessary for the person not to choose any worthless image or think about any negative thoughts or not to choose the path to go down in his life. Because when you think of such images in your mind then your journey will start.

On the physical plane, whether you move or not, but on the mental plane, it has already started. Knowingly or unknowingly this picture will pull your feet in a certain direction and sometimes after walking a few steps you will find that it is very difficult to go back because many things would have changed by walking on these steps so it is important to choose your steps very carefully.

A creative imagination draws energy in a direction where positive vibes surround you. If such imagination is negative, then it will change you in a wrong way and gradually you will find that your nearby surroundings are engaged with such types of negative activities.

Every step counts here and only one picture has enough power to change your life forever. Therefore, choose your picture very carefully, you are not only choosing a picture, but you are also choosing a journey.

8.4 Your Imagination and You

Do not discuss the image of your mind with everyone. No one is interested to know what you are thinking about, according to them all these are only worthless thoughts and you are such a fellow whose brain is stuffed with straws. It is true that people will not pay attention to your words. At the moment, there is only an imaginary picture in your mind, and remember that it is not in the minds of others. If you are putting such a picture into the minds of others then you are making a mistake, because they can see only what is visible in front of their eyes.

Therefore, other than laughing you will not receive anything, it is good to silently work on your path, people who have similar interests soon will join you and people who have no interests will leave you. But you should not stop yourself that you will move when others will come. Preserve your image like a valuable diamond and start working silently and constantly towards the achievement of your goal.

8.5 Imagination is the Key

Imagination is the master key that has the power to open every lock that comes your way as you move forward. Your every action on such a path will strengthen your skills and this will clear the hazy image in your mind. A person always keeps keys in his security and does not discuss them with another person. Your imagination is a key that always needs protection. A person keeps such a key in a very protective area, which means, you should do all work related to your image very carefully and protectively and do not open such a secret to anyone. One day they will know when it becomes a reality, but before that, it is your duty to keep such a key safe with utmost dedication.

8.6 Imagination is a Road Map

A road map helps a person to go in the right direction. Without direction, he will wander around and waste his time and energy. Road maps are available in the market to provide guidance and identify the geographical location. Many people wander around in life without direction, they are looking for a road map, but the road map of life is not available anywhere. The picture you have in your mind is a powerful road map that will save you from wandering around unnecessarily. Such a road map gives you clear guidance on what to do and where to go.

When a person thinks deeply about some image in his mind then his unconscious mind assimilates such image and when something comes from your unconscious mind then it becomes a part of your personality. While sleeping, our unconscious mind remains awake and keeps on working continuously. With the acceptance of the unconscious mind, the change starts and those parts of our brain start functioning which are already dormant. A person having such a road map always takes steps with full caution. They will do concrete planning before taking any step and they will never take any decision in haste because they know that it will take time to travel on such a path.

8.7 Your Imagination Attracts

"Everything is energy and that's all there is to it. Match the frequency of the reality you want and you cannot help but get that reality. It can be no other way. This is not philosophy. This is physics." - Albert Einstein

Always be careful of your imagination, what you imagine you become attracted to it. Take care before selecting a picture, it is going to create an impact on your mind. Every time when you see it, you unconsciously remember it. Unknowingly such attraction is changing you and it is also changing your body language and way of thinking.

Every picture creates an impact on the observer and it gets stored somewhere in our minds. Hence, we never forget what we see anything with our eyes. If we see and think about the image time and again then its visualization is on the top of the mind, we can recall it easily, and whatever the mind recalls it creates an impact on our thinking.

People try to follow the same kind of clothes and style of speaking which makes them feel attracted. Such attraction has a constant effect on our minds and the visuals of such attraction inadvertently alter our body gestures and personality. Therefore, we keep pictures and idols of God in our homes as these images affect us and point our soul toward going to a higher level. The frequent visualization of an image has the potential to change many things in a person's life. Therein lies the ability to completely transform a person and turn his dreams and goals into reality.

Daydreaming turns into powerful imagination when the whole energy of the body is concentrated and the desire to achieve the goal comes from the soul. Then such visualizations start to fuel the image of the mind and the energy starts to do its work and move towards converting it into reality. The unconscious mind starts working in that direction because such visualization reprograms the functioning of the mind and the mind starts working on a new way of thinking.

When you constantly think of an image, your mind accepts it and energy starts running after it to make it come true. Now your mind starts attracting the energy which is needed for it to come true. Castles cannot be built in the air but with such a powerful technique you can build your castle on earth.

As Einstein said, "Everything is energy ……." and now your mind is converting such energy.

Always keep your imagination high in life, this will help you remember that your journey is not over yet. It will provide you an opportunity to hone your skills, such imagination will force you to work hard and keep away from procrastination. The harder you work the picture of your imagination will gradually turn into reality.

<u>Key Points</u>

- ☛ The precision of thinking develops with the power of imagination.

- ☛ Only one image is capable enough to change your life forever.

- ☛ Imagination is the master key that has the power to open every lock which comes on the path.

- ☛ Your imagination is the road map that helps you go in the right direction.

- ☛ What you imagine will attract you and it will change your gesture and the way you think.

- ☛ Always keep your imagination high in life, this will force you to work hard and keep away from procrastination.

Chapter 9

Learning: A Continuous Journey

"Learning is a treasure that will follow its owner everywhere." - Chinese Proverb

Learning is a continuous journey. It is a process that never ends in our life. It also indicates that active energy is working in our body which motivates us to move ahead in life. A child is always curious and wants to know more about the world. He has to go to school and college to learn, without this he cannot move ahead in his life. Being interested in learning generates energy that keeps him agile and active in life. When a person loses interest in learning it indicates that such energy has started to dissipate in his body.

Many people learn only what is necessary for their survival in this world. They have no intention of looking around and discovering anything new in their lives. They want to walk only on those paths which are pre-determined because no intelligence and hard work is required to walk on such paths. Many of them never opened any book after leaving college, they never developed any new skills, they never learn anything new in their life, even many of them never visited any new place because there is also some risk involved. They feel happy because there is no problem in their routine so what is the need to learn something new and take unnecessary risks because every learning has somewhat risked. They say why should I set my mind to learn something new when everything is fine in my life.

But human life is not just to survive on this earth by any means. There is a great meaning behind this life and to discover that we need an evolved soul who is not afraid of circumstances, an active and courageous soul who is not afraid to proceed alone on an unknown path. While traveling on these paths, the circumstances create various problems and they demand timely solutions. Learning is a process that makes a person think and do something more than the mere survival of his life.

A person who is always ready to learn is never afraid of facing any problem. Like a child fall when he starts learning to walk for the first time but soon, he starts running. In the same manner, while learning a skill a person develops such enthusiasm to get up soon and get his desired object. This kind of learning is a never-ending process because once you taste the allure of such enthusiasm you will not be afraid to learn anything new in your life.

The real education of a person begins after he leaves college. College level education is a compulsion, it is known to all that without it they cannot earn a livelihood and cannot move ahead in life. But if a person's goal is only to survive in this world and earn only his livelihood, then he will not take any interest in learning anything new in his life.

Many people earn and live the rest of their lives from what they learn before the age of 25. In later life, they show no interest in acquiring any knowledge and developing any skills. Learning something new or reading a book or acquiring a new skill is just a waste of time for them as they have learned about how to earn their livelihood to survive.

Learning is movement and movement is life. Such movement always enforces the person to remain energetic in his life. A person who is always ready to learn is never disappoints because his life energy is always functioning. When a person learns something and faces such kinds of challenges then there is no meaning to any types of despair and depression in his life because his life has gained momentum.

The success of a person is not judged by how much wealth he accumulates or what designation he holds, but by what qualities he possesses as a better human being. What skills does he have and what kind of thoughts and behavior does he show towards others? The person who has strong human qualities can proceed on the path of creation, this path is not for those who are arrogant and always desirous of power and wealth.

9.1 Always be a Student

Life is a master that never stops teaching us and being a student, we should always follow the direction provided by the master. A person will never feel difficulty in learning and will never be disappointed if he has the qualities of a student, that means;

- A person who is always ready to learn

- A person who is always receptive

- A person who has the curiosity to solve the mystery and is ready to put his energy into that purpose

- A person who is always curious to know and for that purpose is ready to leave his bed and sit at the table at night

Learning from life means not going to college again but a thirst for knowledge which makes a person receptive and only a receptive person can learn easily as his mind does not create any hindrance.

9.2 Nature Supports Learning

Nature supports children to learn, they are energetic, learn quickly and remain active. When a person becomes receptive like a child then he also learns quickly. The person who is always ready to learn is always active and the path of creation requires only an active and receptive person.

9.3 There is No Shortcut to Learning

If you're looking for shortcuts to learn something quickly, you're making a mistake. Learn from your own experience and that is only real learning. On the path of creation, you are not going to crack the exam and get some marks, it is the test of life where you face real challenges that demand real solutions, so, no copy-paste idea works here.

Therefore, never think of taking any shortcut, that others have such skill, talent, resources, etc. and you are behind. You will take the wrong decision if you adopt something like that and ultimately failure will be in your hands. Taking shortcuts is the easiest way to fail.

"One needs to work hard at a steady pace, without being impatient or looking for short cuts, while being

humble even after achieving success. It stresses the need to build a solid foundation to progress further." – **Chinese Proverb**

9.4 No Compulsion to Learn

There is no compulsion to learn from the lessons of life. If you don't want to learn then you can leave it, if you keep repeating the same mistakes again and again in your life, you can do that. If you want to stay in the sleep zone, you can. No one will come and ask you questions and force you that;

- Why are you not learning?

- Why are you not honing your skills?

- Why do you stick to your stereotypes when times are changing?

If you want to leave the path you can, remember there is no compulsion of doing that. A person cannot go on the path of creation by using some force. He will put his energy only if such desire is coming from inside.

9.5 Learning: A Journey That Never Ends

Learning is a continuous journey of life because it always demands development. Learning and exploring new things enhance the knowledge of the person that allows you to continue on the path of creation and success.

The path which is unknown requires many developments and without the zest, you cannot go ahead. After taking only one step many people return from the chosen path because they are afraid of learning which requires time and devotion.

The changing time requires the enhancement of your skill and it is a never-ending process. Life is not static in one place; time is changing continuously and our human body is also. The necessities and resources which seem to be very much essential a few years back and without which we cannot survive become worthless after some time. In the same manner, the knowledge that we learn during our college days demands its development and enhancement. The path to success requires continuous development that is not limited. A person who is ready to learn always remains jovial and such energy does not allow them to sit silent. Learning is joyful and once you experience it you will not be afraid to go ahead alone on the path of creation. Success comes to those who are always ready to learn.

"The great secret of true success, of true happiness, is this: the man or woman who asks for no return, the perfectly unselfish person, is the most successful." - Swami Vivekananda

Key Points

- Learning is a movement that brings hope and enthusiasm.

- A learner must always be receptive.

- A person who is always ready to learn never feels hopeless because his life energy forces him to go for the development.

- There are no shortcuts to learning, taking it is the easiest way to fail.

- A learner is never afraid to go alone because that desire is coming from his soul.

- Success comes to those who are always ready to learn.

Chapter 10

Spiritual Activities

"Spirituality as a science, as a study, is the greatest and healthiest exercise that the human mind can have." - Swami Vivekananda

A person who wants to do something creative in his life must follow spiritual activities in his daily schedule. A person who is saying that he does not have time for prayer means he is not interested in it, he is giving top priority to his worldly activities and is more interested in materialistic desire. Otherwise, it is totally impossible that in 24 hours a person can't find a few minutes for prayer. Such a person is running behind his desire and feels that he is doing something very important in his life and prayer is just a waste of time. But he does not know that the greatest power lies in prayer, an innocent prayer coming from a pure heart never goes in vain.

10.1 Worship Lord Sun

Sun is considered to be the king of the universe. It is a symbol of the Soul and lord of Sunday. The Sun moves in only one direction, never retrogrades, stay in one zodiac sign for one month, and completes the entire zodiac in a year. It is the center of the solar system and everything revolves around the Sun.

Sun is the biggest object and contains 99.8% of the solar system's mass. It is about 150 million kilometres from Earth. Its gravity holds the solar system together. It is not a solid mass; it is composed of layers made up almost entirely of hydrogen and helium. The surface of the Sun is about 10,000 degrees Fahrenheit (5,500 degrees Celsius) hot, while temperatures in the core reach more than 27 million Fahrenheit (15 million Celsius). It has a well-known sunspot cycle which has a maximum of around every 11 years. The Sun is the source of enormous amount of energy, part of which provides the light and heat needed to support life on Earth.

Sun is worshiped among many cultures and in India our Vedas glorified it. We worship Surya as the Sun God, who is the supreme provider and everything on this earth originated from the Sun. In India, on every calendar day of 14th or 15th January, we celebrate Makar Sankranti, when Sun enters in the Capricorn sign. This is the only festival in the country that celebrated on a specific day according to the solar calendar, instead of other festivals which is celebrated as per the lunar calendar.

Sun is the biggest creator of the universe and the source of all life. Sun is known as Aditya, who brings light and warmth, everything that exists on earth comes from the Sun. Without Sun there is no life on earth. It is the Sun who engages the person in their daily activities. Sun not only brightens the day but controls our disposition also.

The person who feels that he himself is controlling his activities and what is the meaning of worshiping Lord Sun as no direct relation is visible in front of his eyes. The person who is chasing after his material desires and does not have time for prayer does not know that in this mundane world, he is doing all those activities because of the Sun. The eyes of such a person are still looking down in the material world and yet he has not looked up which is providing all the energy for our daily activities on the earth.

It is the sun that compels us to rise in the morning and go out into the world. It is the Sun who calls us to wake up every morning and get busy with our work. When the sun rises above the horizon, the morning activities begin to increase and when the Sun moves towards the midheaven, the activities of the people also begin to intensify. At noon, when the Sun is at midheaven then it is very powerful. The activities in the world are also very high during this time. When the Sun slowly starts going down on the horizon, the activities in the world also slow down. At midnight when the Sun is opposite the midheaven point which is called the nadir point, the person goes to bed and falls asleep. Without the Sun there is no activity on earth. It is the Sun that is controlling all the activities of the universe.

Sun controls the atmosphere of the earth. It creates steam and clouds which provides us with water. It is the sun's rays that give a call to the seeds to come out of their shell. All vegetation, trees, and plants make food from the sun's rays, a process called photosynthesis, which is later consumed by other living beings. The sun's rays come to earth to kill bacteria and other harmful viruses and clean the air for breathing and keep us healthy. The sunlight is the main source of the production of vitamin D in our body, reduced exposure to sunlight may cause serious health problems to a person.

Increased exposure to sunlight helps the person to fight off depression. When negative thought starts coming into a person's mind, gradually he starts separation from the outer world. This type of person prefers to sit in a dark room and tries to avoid any kind of light. Actually, he is removing himself from the Sun. Sunlight helps such people to change their thoughts, get energy in their body and come out from the state of darkness. Worshipping Lord Sun removes all kind of darkness from our minds.

- Sun is the soul and worshipping the Lord Sun clears the darkness of the soul.

- Sun gives us light and worshipping the Lord Sun gives us light to our life when we are in a state of complete despair.

- Sun is the source of energy and worshipping the Lord Sun provides us energy and resources.

- Sun removes ignorance and worshiping Lord Sun leads to knowledge. If a person is immersing in the ocean of ignorance, it means that such person is moving away from the Sun by his deeds.

When the sunlight comes everything is visible. The shining Sun in the sky represents strength, energy, and vitality. It represents the power of resistance. It represents mental strength and confidence. It provides courage in a person that the person can go alone in difficult circumstances without any fear. Worshiping Lord Sun enhances many qualities of a person. Hence a person must seek blessings from the greatest creator of the universe for his creation and success.

10.2 Meditation

- **Why should I sit in meditation?**

- **What will I gain by sitting in meditation?**

The above questions start coming into a person's mind when he starts meditating. There are no visible and immediate benefit from meditation and sometimes it takes years to take a dip into meditation. The journey on this path is not easy and only a courageous person can walk on this path. It is the longest journey and travelling on this path completely changes a person.

A person who always thinks about how to get some profit will never sit in meditation, and if he is doing such activities then it is only for showy purposes, he wants to create some impression in his society. Such person may find that while meditating his hands remains empty and time passes.

His mind says what worthless you are doing, go in the world and do some business. Go and attend some party, make some friends and engage yourself in worldly activities. Meditation is only a futile act and a waste of time.

However, a serious person never thinks about what profit I will get if I sit in meditation, obviously, he is getting nothing. The journey on this path requires a tough decision of the person who is not ready to listen to the advice of his mind and ready to search for the light in the deepest darkness. Gradually, the mind starts stabilizing and the turmoil of the brain starts soothing.

In a few instances, the mind says do not go there for meditation, but do not listen to your mind, go and sit silently. Then after few minutes, your mind says that's enough get up and get engage in your business, then do not get up soon, do not listen to your mind again, sit for few more minutes, when you crossed these two obstacles the third obstacle will come, while doing meditation your whole body starts itching and you want to move your hand here and there, this is another trick of the mind which is creating a disturbance in your meditation.

Once you crossed all these hurdles then you start your journey on the path biggest creation. No matter, how many months, years and births will take but your journey has started.

No act in the world is equivalent to meditation, through this the person will change, and change is coming towards the path of light, but he has to pass through the stage of complete darkness, only then he will be able enough to see the light. It takes immense courage to traverse this path and every time your mind tells you to go back, but once you have decided it is fixed forever.

On the path of meditation every drop counts and when you are not in a hurry the result will come quickly and when you are in a hurry it would become longer. Meditation is the greatest creation and no creation in the world is comparable to such a creation.

Key Points

- Every day find a few minutes and sit for prayer.

- Sun is the biggest creator of the universe and worshiping Lord Sun enhances many qualities of a person. One must seek the blessings of Lord Sun every day for his creation and success.

- Sit in meditation without any demand. It is the longest journey and travelling on this path will completely change the life of a person.

Bibliography

Solar system exploration<https://solarsystem.nasa.gov/> Accessed on 6th Feb 2022

<https://www.openbible.info/topics/entering_the_kingdom_of_god> Accessed on 06 March 2022

Happiness <http://www.quoteland.com/topic/Happiness-Quotes/72/ Accessed on 13th March 2022

Warren Buffett Quote<https://libquotes.com/warren-buffett/quote/lbv3b3a> Accessed on 17th March 2022

Scientific Definition <https://www.thoughtco.com/what-is-time> Accessed on 21th March 2022

Energy < https://en.wikipedia.org/wiki/Energy> Accessed on 21st March 2022

Stephen R. Covey <https://www.goodreads.com/quotes> Accessed on 21st March 2022

Quotes by Swami Vivekananda < https://selfdefinition.org> Accessed on 21st March 2022

Storm <https://en.wikipedia.org/wiki/Storm> Accessed on 22nd March 2022

Ramayana story<http://www.bhagavatam-katha.com/ramayana-story-little-squirrel-who-helped-lord-rama/> Accessed on 26th March 2022

Albert Einstein <https://quotefancy.com/quote> Accessed on 4th April 2022

Clapping has Incredible Benefits<https://juniperpublishers.com/ >Accessed on 4th April 2022

Tagoreweb<https://www.tagoreweb.in/Verses/poems-198/if-they-answer-not-3760> Accessed on 9th April 2022

Gautama Buddha < https://www.azquotes.com/quote/667772> Accessed on 16th April 2022

Learning & Development Blog<https://www.dashe.com/blog/motivation/inspiring-learning-quotes/> Accessed on 17th April 2022

Swami Vivekananda Quotes< https://www.highclap.com/inspiring-swami-vivekananda-quotes-thoughts-slogans/> Accessed on 19th April 2022

90 Quotes< https://www.therandomvibez.com/quotes-about-being-humble/> Accessed on 26th April 2022

Culture<https://www.bbc.com/culture/article/20190807-the-women-who-tasted-hitlers-food> Accessed on 30th April 2022

Napoleon Bonaparte <https://www.quotes.net/quote/60998 > Accessed on 1st May 2022

12 Popular Chinese Idioms <https://cudoo.com/blog/popular-chinese-idioms-what-they-mean/> Accessed on 13th June 2022

About The Author

Ajay Srivastava is the founder of lotuswisdom.in and holds 'Bachelor of Science' from Deen Dayal Upadhyay Gorakhpur University, Gorakhpur (UP) and 'Masters Programme in International Business' from PSG Institute of Management, Coimbatore (Tamil Nadu).

He has extensive experience in the capital market as a Lead Analyst, Investment Banker, Consultant, and Advisor in identifying investment opportunities and formulating strategies. In his career, he has written various research notes and has done in-depth research from a commercial and financing point of view in multiple deals. With diverse industry experience and wide understanding, he started imparting his knowledge in the industry since 2013.

He has deep knowledge of graphology and since childhood he is very much interested in analyzing a person by handwriting and has analyzed the handwriting of hundreds of persons in his life.

He is very much passionate to learn about astrology and palmistry in deep and has completed 'JyotirVid' and 'JyotirVisharad' in Astrology from Bharatiya Vidya Bhavan, Mumbai. His various research articles have been published in the renowned magazine "The Astrological eMagazine" and "Planets & Forecast.

Email ID: ajay.srivastava@lotuswisdom.in

Web Site: http://www.lotuswisdom.in/

Books Written by the Author

1. Psychology and Investment

2. Vedic Astrology: The Light of Wisdom

3. Midlife Crisis: An Astrological Approach

4. Jupiter: The Planet of Fortune

5. The Joy of Creation and Success

6. The Light of Nakshatras

7. Sun: The Supreme Creator

8. Astrology & Predictions

9. Animal Symbols of Nakshatras

10. Astrology & Profession

11. Rahu & Ketu: The Invisible & Mysterious Planets

12. Planets & Human Life

<h1 style="text-align:center"><u>Astrology Courses</u></h1>

1. <u>Vedic Astrology for Beginners {Level – 1 (Basics)}</u>

Module – 1: Basics of Astrology

Introduction; The Zodiac; Elements

Module – 2: Signs

Meaning of the Signs, Elements of the Signs, Qualities of the Signs, Odd and Even Signs, Sheershodaya & Prishtodaya Signs, Direction, Colors, Caste, Fruitful and Barren Signs, Masculine & Feminine Signs, Places, Other Major Qualities

Module – 3: Houses

Meaning of the 12 Houses, Types and Classifications of Houses

Module – 4: Planets

Planets and their Characteristics, Planetary Relationship, Exaltation, Debilitation & Mooltrikona, Natural Karakas, Karakas in Jaimini Astrology

Module – 5: Planets in Groups

Natural Benefic and Malefic Planets, Gender; Color; Caste; Guna and Places; Planet and Tastes; Nature of Planet; Elements; Metals; Age; Cloth and Height; Vegetable and Fruits; Physical Constituents and Tendency; Maturity Age of Planets; Planetary Aspects; Seasons; Hora

Module – 6: Planetary Strengths and Weaknesses

Strength of Planets based on its degrees, Direction; Direction Strength; Maran Karaka Sthana; Yog Karaka; Vargottam Planet; Shadabala

Module – 7: Retrograde and Combust Planet, Gandanta

2. <u>Vedic Astrology for Beginners {Level – 2 (Advanced)}</u>

Module 1: Vimshottari Dasha System

Nakshatra and Planetary Lordship, Change of Dasa and Results

Module 2: Basics of Nakshatra

Deity, Animal Symbol, Caste, Activity, Gana, Guna, Gender

Module 3: Important Yogas

Know the 30 most important astrological combinations

Module 4: Ashtakvarga

Interpretation of Ashtakvarga Table

Module 5: Transit of Planets and their impact

Understand the effect of transit of Jupiter, Saturn, Rahu-Ketu

Module 6: Planets and Profession

Identify the influence of the planet and the direction of profession

Module 7: Weak Planets and Remedies

Identify the signal of weak planets and useful remedies

Module 8: Key Steps to Chart Interpretation

Course Offerings:

    · 30 hours of live sessions (Level 1 & Level 2)

    · Learn various astrological concepts with practical examples

    · Mode - Online Classes; Recordings available

3. <u>Nakshatra Course</u>

Knowledge of Nakshatra is very important in astrology, without it one cannot understand how energy works and what will be the result of the transit of planets. Do not limit yourself to the movement of planets, explore the world of Nakshatra and understand the hidden secrets.

What You'll Learn

• How the knowledge of Nakshatra helps to understand the characteristics and negative traits of the person

• Effect of transit of planets and time of activation

• Meaning of each symbol and its influence

• Influence of the associated animal on the personality of the person

• When to start a new venture and when not to go ahead

• Related Profession

• Understand each concept with logic

Course Offerings:

• 60 hours of live sessions

• Learn various astrological concepts with practical examples

• Mode - Online Classes, Recordings available

• Medium - English

Contact Us:

Mobile No.: +91 9867837184

Email ID: ajay.srivastava@lotuswisdom.in

Blog: https://lotuswisdomonline.blogspot.com/

4. A Course on Animal Symbols of Nakshatras

In the ancient scriptures, a total of 14 animals are related to the 27 nakshatras, and the behavior of every person is limited to these 14 animals. To understand the various merits and demerits of a person, it is necessary to understand the different characteristics of these animals.

How to Utilize Such Knowledge

• You will be surprised to know that these animals decide whom we form a relationship in our life.

• These animals determine our relationships with our friends, our spouse, our partners, our juniors and superiors.

• This knowledge helps to channelize your energy in pursuit of higher goals in life.

• The human mind is a very complex creation and it is difficult to say why a person behaves in a certain way and why his behavior changes. Knowledge of animal traits can provide proper guidance in this regard.

Course Offerings:

• 30 hours of live sessions

• Learn various astrological concepts with practical examples

• Mode - Online Classes; Recordings available

Sun:
The
Supreme
Creator
A Research Work on
Astrological Aspects of the Sun
Ajay Srivastava

The Light
of
Nakshatras
A Comprehensive Work to Explain the
Functioning of 27 Mystical Energies
Ajay Srivastava

Jupiter:
The
Planet of
Fortune
Ajay Srivastava

Vedic Astrology
The Light of Wisdom
Astrology for Beginners,
Learn the Language of Stars
Ajay Srivastava

Midlife
Crisis: An
Astrological
Approach
Understand The Timing Of Crisis,
Learn How To Turn A Crisis Into An Opportunity
Ajay Srivastava

PSYCHOLOGY
AND
INVESTMENT
The Art of Investing in Stocks with an
Explanation of Human Psychology
AJAY SRIVASTAVA

The Joy
of
Creation and Success
Ajay Srivastava

Astrology
&
Predictions
Ajay Srivastava

Animal Symbols
of
Nakshatras
Ajay Srivastava

Astrology
&
Profession
Astrological Principles Behind Career
Selection, Downfall and Resurrection
Ajay Srivastava

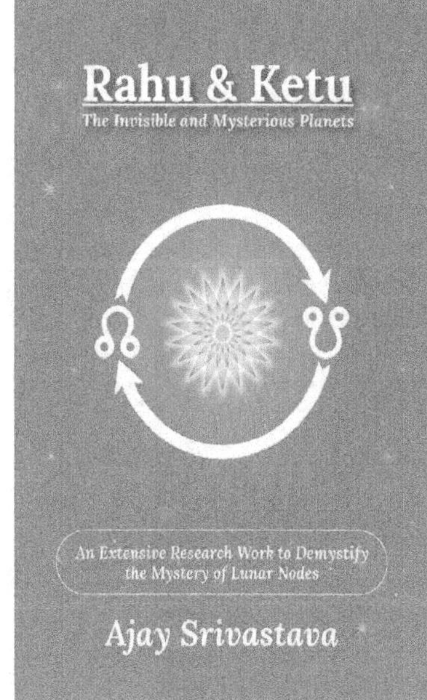

Rahu & Ketu
The Invisible and Mysterious Planets
An Extensive Research Work to Demystify
the Mystery of Lunar Nodes
Ajay Srivastava

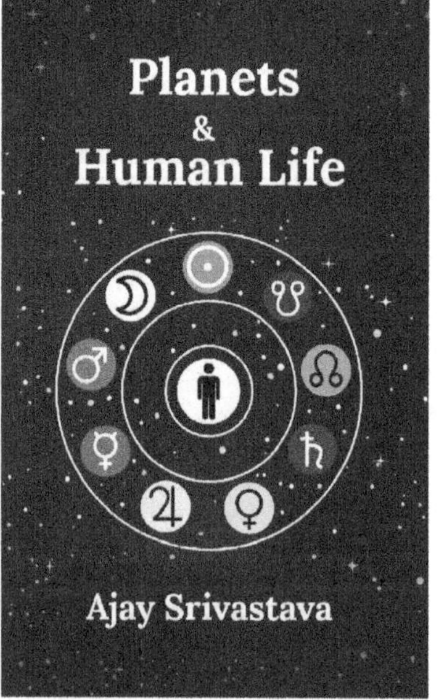

Planets
&
Human Life
Ajay Srivastava

Notes

<u>Notes</u>

Made in the USA
Monee, IL
07 July 2026

56550596R00080